Grandad's Little Stories

STEPHEN JENNINGS FULLER

To my children, their children,
and their children's children.

This little volume is written to save them from having to hear me tell the stories over and over again.

CONTENTS

INTRODUCTION 9

PART ONE

1939 – 1947

Early Years

1. I am happy now — 13
2. Expulsion from primary school — 17
3. The great excuse — 23
4. Lifetime ambitions and God — 27
5. One eyed Dads — 33
6. Stuart and the haircut — 39
7. Father's handwriting — 43
8. Names — 47
9. Time — 53
10. Fuller and the cash labels — 61
11. That side of the water — 67
12. Contentment — 69

13. Gerry Baker and funerals 71
14. Revenge of a wronged Union Hall man 77
15. David and the forge 79
16. The Richard and the Canary islanders 83
17. Fishing 87
18. Farming 95

PART TWO

1947 - 1961

Education

19. Is Cuma liom 105
20. University 111

PART THREE

1961 - 2018

Family

21. The start of married life 121
22. The girls 123
23. The flood in Somerset 131
24. Death of my Father 137
25. Geraldine 143

PART FOUR

1961 - 2019

Career

26. Grandad Stephen John and his grandson Stephen Jennings Fuller	153
27. Hero of the Cold War	161
28. Going to the mountain	169

EPILOGUE: I AM HAPPY NOW II	173

APPENDICES

i	THE FULLERS AND THE MOXLEYS	179
ii	THE FULLER SHOP THROUGH THE AGES	196
iii	TIMELINE OF STEPHEN'S LIFE	199

ACKNOWLEDGEMENTS	201

INTRODUCTION

The world of the 1940s is so different from anything that the young of today can comprehend that I have tried to set the scene and the atmosphere very carefully in ways that mean something to them.

This book is full of my memories and such memories can be inaccurate. My admiration for the place and the people may have resulted in faulty memory. In a few places I have changed names if I thought it might have been somewhat embarrassing. If anybody has information that can add to my memory of incidents in the book I would be delighted to hear from them.

I write these stories not as a history but as a sort of wisdom, so that you, my descendants, will know and appreciate your heritage.

In addition, I have to admit that I get enormous pleasure in writing these anecdotes.

PART ONE

1939 – 1947

THE EARLY YEARS

CHAPTER I

I AM HAPPY NOW

I am 8 years old. I am running down the street on an errand for father. The sun is shining. There is no traffic. There is very little traffic most of the time. I am skipping high and fast. I know only girls skip and I am definitely not a girl. But I exult in skipping high and fast – it makes me feel as if I could fly. I pass the telephone pole outside Dinny Nolan's pub. I bang it with my open hand because I know this causes an echo.

I think, "I am happy now" and then I think, "Will I remember this day?" Perhaps because I asked myself this question I have never forgotten that moment and how I felt.

The year was 1947. The village was Union Hall. My family had been in the village since 1820 and probably before. It is one of the best and most central things in my life that they are still there. I think that brother Stuart is well on his way to creating a dynasty which will enhance the community for many years to come.

Let me try to paint a picture of the village of that time. Union Hall in the 1940s was a very small community. I remember counting the population as 112. None of the houses had electricity or mains gas because there was none in the village. Only three houses had running water and indoor toilets. The Post Office had the only phone. Most houses did not have a radio (wireless as it was called in those days) my guess is that there were less than eight battery operated radios in the whole village.

Transport to and from the village was poor. The nearest bus stop was Leap, 2 miles away and the nearest railway station was Skibbereen, 6 miles away. Most people could only afford taxis (or Hackney cars as we called them) for major events such as weddings or funerals. It was only in 1947 when petrol rationing ended that father was able to use again the car which had been put in storage at the outbreak of war in 1939. Not even any tractors. Consequently most people spent most of their time in the village.

This meant that everybody knew everybody else. Because the population was so small each person was a significant individual in their own right, whatever their age.

Today, the village is very much of the modern world. Communications of all sorts and much greater educational opportunities have made the village a very different place.

And yet it remains the same, populated by interesting and charming people; people who are interested in people. People who respect tradition and family.

A crowd outside Dinny Nolan's pub, with the lamp post, left

CHAPTER II

EXPULSION FROM PRIMARY SCHOOL

In the Ireland of the early 1950s there was a huge division in education. The only Protestant primary school locally was in Corinn - many miles from Union Hall. No public transport was available, but it was out of the question that we three boys would go to the local Catholic school only a mile away.

Irish public opinion at that time did not see this separate schooling issue as prejudice or unusual. It was simply the law of God. It was always thus and would remain so forever. Catholics went to Catholic schools and Protestants went to Protestant schools. The logic behind this apparent nonsense was the Roman Catholic Church's edict that the non RC partner of a Catholic had to "turn" to Roman Catholicism or at the very least that the children of such a marriage be brought up as Roman Catholics. Minority Christian religions saw that this edict would inevitably lead to the extermination of their branch of the faith within a few generations if young people were to marry those with whom they mixed socially – the solution, as they saw it, was to have as little social interaction as possible. No other religions were of significance in the rural Ireland of those days. One *heard* that there were Jews but they were very few in number and anyway lived in big cities such as far away Dublin and Cork.

So what were my parents to do about primary schooling for their three sons?

In Skibbereen 6 miles away there was a private Protestant kindergarten run by a very genteel lady, Miss Swanton. Skibbereen had the great advantage in that every morning a 'mail car' brought the post to Union Hall and in the afternoon the mail car collected the post from Union Hall to take to the Skibbereen depot. Thus for a relatively small amount of money we boys could travel with Pete 'the mail car man' in his tiny Ford Popular. Luckily Pete was small, we were only small boys, and there were only two small post bags and a few parcels so we all fitted in – just.

I must have been a sore trial to Miss Swanton. I could not see the point of school. Why bother waste time reading? It was not nearly as much fun as the glorious playground that was Union Hall and our shop and the various stores full of places I could climb and explore. I was aggressive, hugely energetic, really not interested in school activities, barely able to read or write and unable or unwilling to behave as she expected her pupils to behave. The only way she could get anywhere with keeping me reasonably quiet was to have competitions such as spelling tests and our times tables. Unfortunately this was not enough to prevent me from being a disruptive influence.

After a couple of years, a new boy came to the school. Red was not a very talented boy but large for his age, which was a year or so older than I. Red's self-esteem was bolstered by pushing the smaller kids around. Even though we were about the same age I was noticeably smaller. Red probably reckoned that there were more vulnerable targets than me so he left me alone. Stanley however, aged 4, was an easier target.

One day on the way home, Stanley was bruised and crying. I discovered that Red was the cause of the problem. As the older brother it was *clearly* my responsibility to sort the matter out. But how? Awkward and clumsy Red might be, but he was so much bigger than me.

Pete's times were dictated by his responsibilities to the Mail Service, so we always arrived for school half an hour or more before it opened. When we arrived the next morning I saw that the coalman had delivered a load of open coal for storing in the cellar. Here was my answer because luckily Red was early too. As he came up the drive he was greeted by a fusillade of lumps of coal which I was hurling at him from atop the heap. Red retreated howling, I was victorious!

When Miss Swanton was told of my crime she was strangely quiet. The consequences were twofold; one Red never hit any of the Fullers again. Two, a few days later Father informed me that he had agreed with a letter he had received from Miss Swanton, which advised him "to take Stephen from her school and send him to somewhere larger which would be more appropriate for his educational requirements."

Thus I went to Bandon Grammar School as a boarder aged eight and a half. Apparently I cried for 20 minutes after Mother dropped me off but after that I enjoyed school as much as anybody I have ever spoken to.

I like to say that I am the only person I know who was expelled from their primary school. Strictly speaking I was not expelled - but I nearly was.

CHAPTER III

THE GREAT EXCUSE

This story may contain an attitude to meat eating and child rearing which is not in accord with some of today's society. However, it does accurately reflect the prevailing attitudes of the rural Ireland of that time. If you fear you may be offended, please move to the next story.

As I go through life I hear so many excuses. They can be irritating, as what happened to me this morning; the lady in the pharmacy forgot my prescription and fell back on the old one: "The computer crashed". Idiotic; as when the politician always blames the other side. Annoying or funny (depending on the circumstances); as when my younger grandchildren pout "well, he hit me first!" But the silliest excuse I have heard was made by me.

In the spring of 1944, when I was aged 5, Stuart was 3 and Stanley was a plump unsteady on his feet toddler, there occurred a reasonably rare event; Father arranged for the slaughter of a pig in our backyard.

This killing of a pig may seem very odd in the 21st Century. Today I can imagine people protesting at the cruelty of it all. Many a vegetarian would be horrified. Virtually everybody, in this day of plastic vacuum-packed bacon would say, "Why would anybody do such a thing?"

However in rural 1944 Ireland it made a whole lot of sense. Food rationing prevailed. The Department of Agriculture banned all production of meat except through controlled licensed premises. So anybody who could supply really good meat which was not rationed was sure of a good demand, thus enhancing their already good reputation of being an excellent grocer.

The yard was prepared. A large bench was produced on which the protesting pig was to be put. Knives were sharpened. The enthusiastic but rather inexperienced butchers were arrayed in aprons and wellington boots. The yard gate was locked in case nosey neighbours – or worse, a member of the Department of

Agriculture – happened by.

I cannot remember the whole of this episode. Mother used to tell the story with glee for many years so I am not sure which part I remember and which part I fill in from her story. I do remember that I was hugely excited at the great event. I can recall the sense of tension, the squealing of the pig, the blood gushing from its throat (which was carefully stored for the later production of black pudding).

I can remember Mother saying to me: "Stephen, you must look after Stanley. See that he does not get his feet wet". I should explain that outside our backdoor was a very large Belfast sink whose function was to provide a reservoir of drinking water from which the dogs and the cows drank. It was also the best place for three unruly small boys to sail their boats in and splash one another and indeed do what other mischief we could think of. What Mother meant was that I should ensure the toddler Stanley was not allowed to play with the water. After all he was still only saying a few words and was really not capable of looking after himself.

I got hugely engrossed in the spectacle of the pig. This was high drama. This was grown up stuff.

I was brought back to my responsibilities very quickly when the cry went up, "Look at the baby!"

Everyone turned around to see that the only visible part of small toddler Stanley was his feet waving in the air above the surface of the water in the Belfast sink. Amid much hullabaloo he was rescued. Towelled down, the centre of attention and slightly bewildered, Stanley was the subject of much hugging and kissing. I was ignored which, given the circumstances, suited me nicely. I was about to make myself scarce when Mother, rather unfairly I thought, attempted to put the blame on me. I came up with The Great Excuse.

"You told me to keep his feet dry and they are. Look!"

CHAPTER IV

LIFETIME AMBITIONS AND GOD

My paternal grandmother Anne (Annie) Vickery was a very remote lady but central in my earliest memories. She and her youngest daughter, Doris, who had epilepsy, shared our house. Granny Fuller and Doris, although they lived under the same roof as us, led almost entirely separate lives to my parents. I do not know why but we never, for instance, shared a meal. Granny Fuller and my parents never quarrelled in my presence but they were quite distant to one another. Granny and Doris had their own suite of rooms, bedroom, kitchen, dining room, sitting room and bathroom.

As a small boy I saw nothing unusual in this. I accepted it as a law of the universe and never asked questions. I moved between the two worlds. I thought then and others have told me since, that I was really rather a favourite of Granny Fuller. I certainly spent much more time with her than Stuart or Stanley did. When I finally learned to read, she had me read to her. Much of it, I am afraid, from the Bible and similar theological stories. I did not find it interesting but again I accepted it as another law of the universe that this is what I had to do.

The family had been divided along religious lines. Granny Fuller's family, the Vickerys, had been staunch Methodists and Granny remained so. On the other hand, Grandfather Stephen's family had been Church of Ireland (Anglican). After their marriage Grandfather Stephen seemed to drift into the Methodist church and their children were all brought up as Methodists. To us today the division between Methodism and Anglicans may seem very minor. However, the divisions were enormous to the devout of either belief in those days. When Father married Mother as a member of the Church of Ireland, he did so in a church of the Church of Ireland. He and Mother and we kids went to the Church of Ireland. In later years Father was elected a member of the General Synod (Parliament) of the Church of Ireland, to his great amusement because officially he was not even a member of the Church of Ireland, since he had been brought as a Methodist and never officially changed from that.

I remember very clearly the day when Granny called me into her dining room; a dark sombre room furnished with dark silks and dark wood, the only real light coming from the polished silver. That room had always rather intimidated me. Granny, without any introduction, said: "Stephen, I want you to become a Methodist minister: If you do, I will pay all your schooling fees and expenses and I will leave all my money to you."

Looking back it seemed strange that she made no attempt to sell me the idea, no attempt to elaborate on what she meant, she was as blunt and as short as I have related. I remember my reply very clearly: I said (and I quote), "Granny, even though I am only 8 years I know that there are three things in life that I do not want to be. I do not want to be a Methodist minister, I do not want to be a shopkeeper, and I do not want to be a doctor." I didn't want to be a shopkeeper because father was a shopkeeper and often bemoaned his lot. Looking back, I think he had rather a good life. I don't know why I said I didn't want to be a doctor but I sense it was because the local GP held a surgery once a week and on the few occasions that I passed the door into the street, the room was extremely crowded and extremely smelly.

Granny Fuller was a very good looking lady as can be seen in the lovely photograph of her with her husband Stephen John (I have always thought that she is where Brother Stuart got his good looks from. Certainly there is a significant likeness) however unlike Stuart she was remote and stern. I cannot remember her smiling even once.

I thought nothing more about it but she never attempted to raise the subject again. I wonder why when in fact she had been talking to a child only 8 years old. When you consider the grasp of the world that most 8 year olds have, I think that if I had been her I would have raised the subject on other occasions with a view to getting a more favourable answer. However, I remain very clear, she wouldn't have succeeded anyway.

She kept her implied promise and did not leave me, or indeed my siblings, a single penny.

***

Talking about religion reminds me of another occasion when it came into my life.

I was 14 years old, I had many things going for me. For instance, I was driving a car on my own and nobody prevented me, with our village being so remote. However, I was sorely tried because I was *very* small for my age and this bothered me.

Even though Stuart my brother was 18 months younger than me, he was already significantly taller than me, not only taller but heavier and generally a much finer athlete. Because I was reasonably bright I was in a class of which the average age was 2 years older than I. Thus I was 2 years younger than most people and I was small for my age - so in class photos. I appear miniscule. Indeed I have one picture in which my head just reaches Peter Anderson's shoulder, and only Ed Bird's elbow!

I made a deal with God.

God, if ever I get to be 5ft 10 inches and 10 stone I will always be a good person.

I regret to say that God kept his side of the bargain and gave me amongst many other blessings 6ft and 12+ stone but I have many times let Him down.

Nowadays I think God may be getting His own back. Due to my advancing years and a major operation when I was 72 my height has shrunk to 5 feet 9 inches. I still weigh over 12 stone so perhaps my additional girth makes up for my reduction in height.

Grandmother Anne Fuller (nee Vickery) loved to swim. Seen here at Squince in 1930

CHAPTER V

ONE EYED DADS

When I was little I believed that all Dads had only one eye fixed in their head. Dads took out their other eye before going to bed, then carefully put it in a glass in the bathroom. In the morning Dads just popped that eye back in. I must have been six or seven years old before I heard the real story.

As a young man, Father was a very keen sportsman: rugby, fishing, collecting birds' eggs and shooting wild game such as duck, usually mallard, sometimes teal, rarely widgeon. Pigeons and crows were a menace to the vegetable garden and to the crops on the farm so they too had to be kept to a minimum. Snipe, a small, very fast, bird with a darting flight and constant changes of course were particularly difficult targets. Unlike today, beautiful woodcock were quite numerous. However the biggest and rarest prize in father's rough shooting days were pheasant.

Today pheasant are abundant. However the pheasant that we see now are virtually all hand reared and then set free by specialist gamekeepers. It is an expensive business caring for and feeding these birds. In those days the pheasant was rare in West Cork. The birds that were there had been hand reared in some of the more affluent counties in the midlands and somehow a very small number of these pheasant found their way to West Cork.

The pheasant is an unusual bird in that it does not really like to fly. When it does fly, it flies only short distances. When disturbed, its mode of escape is to run rapidly in short bursts. Faced by a hedge it flaps its wings at a great rate creating a terrific noise and hullabaloo – even then it creates only just enough momentum to clear a hedge.

Father was a 28 year old bachelor when he went shooting one morning, he was a bit disturbed because his number one shotgun was at the gunsmiths being serviced and his gundog was ill. His dog was an excitable youngster; in many ways a hindrance because he got so excited. The gun he had that day was an old one which his father had used and which at some stage had had an accident whereby a heavy weight had fallen on and dislodged the trigger guard. The trigger guard is a metal U shaped loop which helps to prevent the triggers being accidentally pulled. Good shooting practice calls for a number of security precautions. One of the most fundamental precautions is to "break" the shotgun whenever one is in any potentially risky situation. "Breaking" means opening the catch which holds the shotgun together so that one can put in or take out the cartridges. When broken the gun cannot be fired because the detonating pins are removed from all possible contact with the cartridges.

This particular morning Father was shooting above Kilbeg. He was enjoying the glorious views over the inner harbour. Then his reverie was disturbed by the sight of a pheasant scuttling along the ground. Good manners/protocol prevents one from shooting a bird on the ground. Father, greatly excited, gave chase so that the bird would take to the air. The pheasant ran through a gap in the hedge. Father followed. The pheasant faced with another hedge with only a small gap, rose into the air with a huge flurry of flapping wings and noise. Father going through the gap was much too excited to take the time to break the gun. A bramble caught in one of the triggers. The gun went off. The lead shot ricocheted off the stone-hedge. Father felt a huge pain in his right eye.

The local Doctor could do nothing. Father was rushed 50 miles to Cork to the Royal Victoria Hospital, where the eye was deemed hopeless and so it was removed.

Father's convalescence was greatly improved by the charming nursing sister. Luckily, she reciprocated his feelings, and they married.

So that is how my brothers and I, our 10 children, and our grandchildren – all 21 of them - originated.

A potentially fatal accident, certainly a stupid accident led to all these people.

Every cloud has a silver lining.

Martha Fuller (nee Jennings) as a Nurse at Victoria Hospital, Cork

Noel Fuller

CHAPTER VI

STUART AND THE HAIRCUT

When we were little boys, adults used to coo with admiration over Stuart's glorious blond curly hair. Apparently I was jealous and talked about my curls. The reality was I had sticky up, absolutely straight hair. To make matters worse, the colour was a shade of red that the locals called foxy and was much despised.

Din Minihane was a local fisherman who had the luck and sense to give up the hard work, erratic income and the very real danger which sea fishing entailed for a cushy job as gardener to a kindly old lady member of the gentry, Mrs Travers of Glandore. Din was a gentle, intelligent man of many skills - one of which was cutting hair for his male friends and neighbours.

When he came to earn some extra income helping Mother with her gardening, he would also cut Father's hair. When we children came along, he would also cut our hair.

Din's hairdressing equipment was basic – a pair of scissors, a comb and a couple of manually operated hair trimmers (remember we had no electricity to use powered trimmers). His 'salon' was the kitchen. His barber's chair was a dining room wooden carver chair in which adults sat. Kids were put on a board resting on the arms of the carver to raise them to a height which was comfortable for Din to reach.

Mother used to tell the story of how one day Din cut Father's hair, then mine, then Stuarts and finally he turned his attention to 15 month old Stanley. Apart from a gentle trimming by Mother using a scissors to just tidy up his baby locks, Stanley had never had a proper haircut. Stanley really did not like being sat on a wobbly board with a strange man pushing him around, so he did what any sensible infant would do.

He screamed.

He hollered.

He shook his head frantically to keep this strange man away from him.

He continued this frenzy so that Mother, Father and Din were really focussed on trying to calm him.

Apparently I, realising that the adults were occupied elsewhere, persuaded Stuart that I was going to practise hair cutting on him. 2 ½ year old Stuart sat on a kitchen chair whilst, using one of Din's trimmers, 4 year old Stephen cut a path up the middle of Stuart's glorious blond hair.

I do not remember most of the events described. However even now I can see very clearly the 2 inch wide crew cut swathe in the middle of Stuart's beautiful hair.

Jealousy is a green eyed monster.

CHAPTER VII

FATHER'S HANDWRITING

Father and his brothers Tom and Bill were given their secondary school education at Methodist College Belfast, usually called Methody or MCB. His sisters Nancy and Mabel went to Wesley College, Dublin. I do not know about his sister Doris – her epilepsy may have prevented her going to boarding school.

They were given their primary education by a private tutor. I know nothing of this person, however the tutor must have been relatively enlightened because they allowed the left handed members of the family to learn to write with their left hands. Methody was more draconian and everybody had to write with their right hand. Subsequently Father used to boast that he could write with either hand. Indeed one of his party tricks was to write with both hands simultaneously.

The reality was that his handwriting was so awful that it might be said that he could not write. His writing was barely legible and appeared more similar to the Nasta'liq script used in Persian calligraphy of the 15th and 16th century than to the Latin alphabet.

When I got letters from home during my school days I had to rely on educated guesses to work out what a lot of the words were.

The odd thing was that no typewriters were used in the business and Union Hall did not have any telephones except in the Post Office until 1948 so he had to order his goods by post. Goodness knows how the suppliers were able to read his writing.

An example of Father's handwriting

CHAPTER VIII

NAMES

Father's younger brother William Vickery Fuller was usually called Bill by the time I knew him. Lucky really, because during his childhood everybody had called him Willie. Indeed many of his childhood contemporaries still called him Willie. However his formidable English wife Gwen had decreed that he be called Bill. And so Bill he became. We smutty minded children rather liked him and so were pleased that we did not have to call him Uncle Willie.

Uncle Bill and Aunty Gwen stayed with us often. Bill had various jobs in the Empire. From Cambridge he went directly to what was then called the Gold Coast (nowadays Ghana). Immediately after getting his degree from Cambridge he was appointed Assistant

District Commissioner in the Colonial Service in the Gold Coast with responsibility for over a ¼ million people. He was posted up river in an area where not another white man resided. He later told me that he was Chief of Police, Chief Magistrate, Chief Prosecutor and Head of the Civil Service in his area at the age of 22. There were no white women allowed because it was decreed that white women could not survive in that tropical lowlands climate, accordingly Aunty Gwen did not accompany him.

In later years Bill was a District Commissioner attached to the British mandate in Palestine until 1948 when the British withdrew. Palestine at that time was a hotbed of violence so again Aunty Gwen could not live there with him.

Anyway, Aunty Gwen who suffered from delusions of grandeur and a husband with a small income decided that she could overcome the latter and feed the former by attaching herself to the Fuller household in Union Hall for months at a time. She expected to be and, it seemed to me, was treated like a member of the aristocracy.

Uncle Bill got leave for six months every two years. On one of the early periods of leave Aunty Gwen said to him that she had been talking to Mrs. O'Donovan, Uncle Bill enquired which Mrs.

O'Donovan?

The lady who lived next door was Mrs. O'Donovan, but the lady who lived next door on her left was also Mrs. O'Donovan, and the lady who lived next door on *that* lady's left was also Mrs. O'Donovan, and the lady who lived next door on *that* lady's left was Mrs. O'Donovan. Indeed half the ladies in the village were called Mrs. O'Donovan.

This profusion of O'Donovans led to unusual ways of identifying which was the O'Donovan in question. The normal way was to give the first name but here again there were complications caused by having only a limited selection of first names.

Mary and Bridget were the names most often used for girls and John, Patrick, and Michael were often used as boys' names. Plus of course the variants such as Bridie, Breege, Breda, Breed. Somebody christened Patrick could in common usage be called Pat, Patsy, Paddy, Paudge or Padraig.

So describing somebody as Mrs. Mary O'Donovan was no help because there were so many Mrs. Mary O'Donovans. You could describe the person as Mary Patrick O'Donovan which helped a bit because you knew she was Mary daughter of Patrick. It often did not help a lot because there were a lot of Marys who had a father called Patrick. So one had to move another generation as in Mary Mikey Micky.

Addresses did not help because the addresses were usually Union Hall. Nor did occupation help much because there were very few jobs available other than farming, fishing or labouring.

There were exceptions however. One kindly person who was a particular favourite of mine was Timothy Bridget.

In those days there was a huge anxiety to get Catholic children baptised early in case they died. Newborn babies were taken immediately to the Church for baptism by the Priest. The Mother having just given birth did not attend. There was also a custom of 'wetting the baby's head' which, I seem to remember, meant the new Father buying drinks all round.

Timothy Bridget's birth was a very drawn out affair. So long drawn out in fact that the men of the family and their neighbours got bored of waiting and started 'wetting the baby's head' before Timothy Bridget appeared. They did this to such good effect that they were very happy. Timothy Bridget eventually was born and was taken, wrapped in swaddling clothes, to the church to be christened by the Priest.

The baby was duly christened and was brought back triumphantly to the Mother who asked what name the child had been given.

The reply came, "Timothy of course, our great family name." The mother was aghast because, as she pointed out, the baby was a girl.

Consternation. What to do?

They trooped back to the church and admitted the mistake to the Priest asking him to change the name. The Priest very reasonably replied that he had already signed the Official Register of Births and there was no way such an official entry could be changed.

Then inspiration struck the priest. The entry in the Official Register of Births could not be changed but *it could be added to*...Timothy had been entered in the left hand side of the page but another name could be added on the same line after Timothy. Another Christening took place and hence Timothy Bridget.

A lovely name for a really lovely person.

***

Aunty Gwen was involved in another story about names.

On one of her visits she accompanied us to Church. Going into Church she saw a lady she remembered having met on a previous visit but about whom she could not remember very much. During the service Gwen worried about what to say when they would meet outside the church.

The more she thought about the lady the more she remembered: *lived locally... aspirations of being the 'gintry'... very nice - but with a loud piercing Anglo-Irish accent... her husband ex-British Army, but what was the name? Aha! Got it! Mrs Brazier Creagh... must not forget it, but how to remember? Brazier Creagh... 'Crazy bray'... DO NOT call her that! Mrs Brazier Creagh...*

After Church we stopped to chat in the sunshine of the lovely gravel yard of Glandore Church with its wonderful view of the bay. Aunty Gwen said loud and clear, "Good Morning, Mrs. Crazy Bray!"

CHAPTER IX

<u>TIME</u>

When I muse contentedly with my memories I often draw parallels between stories of my childhood and modern life. However, there are some items which are so different that I cannot envisage anything like this happening today. For example, I always chuckle to myself when I remember the jennet.

Most people know what a mule is. However, for those who do not know, a mule is:

1. The offspring of a male donkey and a female horse, typically sterile

2. A hybrid plant or animal, especially a sterile one

3. An obstinate person or animal

However, most people do not know what a jennet is. A jennet is:

1. The offspring of a male horse (usually a pony which is a small horse) and a donkey

2. or a mule

3. An obstinate person or animal but much more so than a mule

My granny Fuller, that is my father's mother, owned a jennet. Taller than your average donkey of a grey brown colour with mean, rather vindictive eyes. It led what seemed a rather pointless existence.

Father always had a horse or sometimes two. The horses were used for ploughing and, up to about 1947 when private motor driven vans were allowed on the road again, were used to make local deliveries and draw goods from the nearest railway station in Skibbereen. These horses were usually amiable and relished the apples, carrots and mangles we gave them as treats. They also allowed us to ride them. The jennet however had no such inclination.

It wasn't only children that the jennet did not like: He disliked everybody, especially the person who was unlucky enough to be asked by Granny Fuller to harness it to her small trap, a two-wheeled carriage.

Now they had to persuade the jennet to move and to move in the direction in which Granny wanted to travel. There were only a limited number of destinations which Granny wished to go. The jennet knew and disliked them all. Some of these it disliked even more than others, especially those that involved travel uphill.

The jennet always battled with my strong minded Granny. Granny usually won the battle of wills and they would eventually set off, albeit at a slow pace with stops and starts.

The jennet knew exactly the point at which the journey became the homeward leg. His tail erect, he trotted quickly and proudly for home. Granny claimed that although the journey home was covered quickly he was always careful and did not take risks.

When he died aged 39 we all missed him. We missed him as a character but not with affection.

***

One of Granny Fuller's favourite destinations for her journeys with the jennet was Tralaan. Although only half a mile along the coast from Squince, in those days the only access to Tralaan was by a narrow unmade deeply rutted road down a steep slope where it got too steep.

Granny and Doris would tether the jennet in a little area where the road widened and walk the remaining couple of hundred yards. I remember being with them as we staggered under loads of rugs, swimming things, a vacuum flask of tea, homemade lemonade, sandwiches, biscuits, things to read, etc. Granny swam in the sea as often as she could for at least nine months a year. Doris was not so brave but she did for perhaps six months.

Here they could stay for hours rarely talking but contentedly and slowly swimming, eating, drinking, reading the church magazine and religious tracts. Once I had learned to read I was expected to read aloud to Granny from the Bible but the Bible was considered too heavy to take on our excursions so I read from the religious tract with Granny very diligently correcting my pronunciation.

Tralaan beach was a very good place to gather Carrageen Moss (a form of seaweed) which she would pick, dry in the sun, boil it in milk and then made it into a jelly. Extremely nutritious and good for one. She and Doris loved it. The only drawback for me was that

I found it tasted terrible.

***

Near Tralaan, one of Granny's favourite beaches, lived two brothers who were special to my childhood. Paddy and Tadgh 'the Island'. I remember Paddy as being old in my childhood eyes (must have been at least 40) and Tadgh must have been maybe 20 years older.

They lived in a lovely cottage with surely one of the loveliest views in the world; the glorious Rabbit Island with its gravel beaches and precipitous cliffs, and in the middle distance the magnificent High Island with its neighbour Low Island further away. To the west Squince beach and beyond to Myross Island and to the east the majestic sweep of Clonakilty Bay with the Galley Head lighthouse on the tip of the peninsula.

The brothers earned their living lobstering and fishing. Lobstering is the term used when catching lobsters in a pot made, in those days of a willow frame and netting (today the willow is often replaced with a lightweight non-corroding metal). The brothers fished using hand lines.

When Father took us fishing this area was one of his favourite fishing grounds. Any time we saw the brothers, we always waved or spoke to them as they rowed their 18 foot yawl.

Paddy and Tadgh were wonderful oarsman, seemingly and effortlessly rowing with all the elegance of ballet dancers. Graceful, stylish and so beautiful. Odd words to use about two middle aged fishermen. Odd but true.

There is a lovely story told about Paddy and whether true or not, I have always enjoyed it. Apparently, when he was a young man perhaps 18 or so, he came to the village to do some shopping. As a special treat Paddy went to the sweetie shop. Alas the lady who owned the sweet shop was not there. However, her young assistant was.

Paddy asked for his favourite sweets but did not know the name or brand. He and the young assistant decided that some brightly coloured sweets in a jar were probably the ones he usually had. So Paddy treated himself to six pennorth. You got a lot of sweets for a penny in those days so he got a sizeable bag... Paddy had his first sweet and realised that they were different from his usual ones but, nevertheless, they tasted really good.

After he had concluded his business in the village and chatted to his friends Paddy headed homewards. He went up past the Black

Field and had just got to the Chapel when he had a huge urge to answer a call of nature. Quick as a flash he was over the ditch taking his trousers down. He resumed his journey but had not got very far when he had another huge urge. He narrowly avoided a catastrophe and gingerly started for home again. This went on and on for the next couple of miles.

He was fed up, tired and worried about this repeated urge to hop over the hedge and do the necessary undressing. When he got to within half a mile of his home there were very few houses about. Apparently, he eventually decided to save time by trudging home just carrying his trousers.

Sometime later it was discovered that the 'sweets' he had been sold were old fashioned laxatives!

Stephen, Stuart and
Stanley Fuller as boys

CHAPTER X

FULLER AND THE CASH LABELS

Our parents chose names for us on a very logical basis which I shall explain before telling you why their logic led to a lot of trouble and an ingenious solution.

I was christened Stephen because not only Father and Grandfather were Stephen but there appeared to be a line of Stephen Fullers going back for centuries. I was given Jennings as a second name because of the Northern Irish and Scottish custom of giving a child the Mother's maiden surname as a Christian name.

Stuart was called George Stuart because George was a Vickery name, our paternal Grandmother was a Vickery. Where Stuart came from I forget but it did not matter anyway because he was to be called George.

Stanley was called Thomas Stanley because a very popular Fuller first name was Thomas. Again I do not know where Stanley came from but it did not matter because he was going to be called Tom anyway.

Unfortunately (and I know not why) George and Thomas did not stick, my brothers were always called Stuart and Stanley.

Now this is where the trouble began: You had three siblings whose names all began 'St'.

Mother had the same affliction I have inherited – an inability to remember names. This meant that when Mother wanted to call us for one reason or another she would shout, "Stephen come here." Louder: "No, Stuart come here." Bellowed: "Oh bother, Stephen, Stuart, Stanley come *here*."

Trouble arose in our teenage years (long before mobile phones) when letters in girl's handwriting would arrive home during the school holidays addressed to Mr. S. Fuller.

When we went to Bandon Grammar School the Headmaster Ivan McCutcheon was equally confused by our names. He sorted the problem by calling us Fuller I, Fuller II and Fuller III.

Every item of school clothing had to be marked with the pupils' name which meant Mother had a cupboard full of name tags for us. Mr. McCutcheons' unusual naming plan was a help to her in this regard. From then on she ordered only Fuller III nametags. Stanley got the name tag in full Fuller III, Stuart got the name tag slightly folded back on itself Fuller II and I got the name tag even more folded back on itself to read Fuller I.

***

Talking about names reminds me of an entirely different story. Attendance at church on Sundays was not optional. Sometimes one got a choice of which church service to attend but *not* going to church on a Sunday was entirely out of the question.

Glandore church was, and is, a truly beautiful building in tranquil surroundings. Set in a niche in the living rock, the small church looks out over the beauty of Glandore Bay. The Fuller family pew had a South facing window through which the sun streamed on a summer morning. Early on in my church going I decided that the seat next to the window was mine. Here I could look out on one of the most beautiful views in all of God's Earth.

In these circumstances, Brother Stanley tended to find church services sleep inducing, and he often found a comfortable position to drift off.

On one such occasion Canon Colthurst was delivering a sermon, the theme of which, I know not. However it included reference to the missionary Dr. David Livingstone and the search for him by the British explorer Henry Stanley.

A small rather quiet man, Canon Colthurst's sermons were usually delivered in a non-controversial monotone. On this occasion however the good Canon got caught up in the drama of Dr. Livingstone being discovered in the jungle.

The Canon exclaimed loudly the explorer's surname "Stanley!" and paused for effect.

In the silence that followed a drowsy Stanley was heard to say in the ringing tones we were required to use for school attendance roll calls "Here Sir!"

***

Another Story about Stanley, church and sleep

Miss Johnson was a gentle spinster lady who lived a genteel existence in Ballincolla House, a mile or so from our house and a few hundred yards from Kilbeg. She had a decent sized house and garden on the water's edge set in 30 acres. A couple of servants and, sometimes, a companion completed the picture.

In 1950, Miss Johnson was about 70, I was 11, Stuart 9 and Stanley 7 or thereabouts. Miss Johnson did not have a car, in fact we were one of the few houses in the area with a car. Miss Johnson used to come to church in Union Hall (I think by walking) however, it was too far to walk when the service was in Glandore so we would give her a lift.

Miss Johnson sat in the front passenger seat whilst we three imps sat in the back directly behind her. Miss Johnson arrayed for a Church service was a regal sight. Fur hat with a veil, fur coat, large brooches and clinking jewellery. Her hair however was what fascinated us boys. Voluminous glistening brown coils emerged from beneath her hat.

We had overheard an adult say that it might be a wig. The speculation was exciting and endless. How would we find out?

One Sunday Stanley, as often, fell asleep during the sermon. This time he sprawled even more awkwardly than usual, causing some shuffling in the crowded pew. Emerging from church Stanley hissed excitedly for Stuart and I to follow him to a corner of the church yard. There he confided to us that he had solved the problem.

Miss Johnson's hair was indeed a wig. Awaking from his pretend slumber, he had 'accidentally' pulled her hair which dislodged and slid over her left eye.

CHAPTER XI

THAT SIDE OF THE WATER

Union Hall in the 1940s and 1950s was remote from the rest of Ireland and certainly from the rest of the World. A journey to the nearest big town Skibbereen (population 1700), was a rare event.

Today we are connected globally. Telephones, email, computers, television, foreign travel, and more years of formal education mean that people in Union Hall and its parish of Myross are aware of people and events in faraway places. Not so back then.

Once, Stuart and I were making the weekly delivery to Patsy Murray, who had a small farm near Myross School, about a mile west of the village. The year must have been about 1950 because I had been driving without a license since I was 12. The delivery was probably Patsy's usual requirements: A couple of hundred weight* bags of pig meal, maize (which we called Indian meal) used as cattle feed, bran meal, coal, two gallons of paraffin for lamps and his weekly very basic groceries.

As usual Patsy enquired what the latest news was. This was quite a customary question from our customers because they saw a shopkeeper as having a central role in the community and therefore would know the latest gossip. I replied that old Miss Mongo had died. Patsy said that he did not know her. I said, "Of course you must be Patsy, she is the sister of Paddy O'Donovan whom we call Paddy Mongo… They live just on the other side of the bridge to Glandore" (which was a distance of about a mile from the village in the opposite direction to where Patsy lived).

Patsy dismissed my reply: "Oh, I wouldn't know anybody from that side of the water." He clearly had no knowledge of or interest in anybody who lived at most 2 miles away from him. He looked on such people as being outside his area. At age 60 he had probably not been "that side of the water" more than half a dozen times in his life.

---

*a hundred weight, written cwt., equals 8 stone or 112 pounds or 51 kilograms

CHAPTER XII

CONTENTMENT

At the end of the village opposite the Quay lived another Patsy Burke. Quiet. Gentle. A bachelor. Short, slim and slightly stooped, Patsy kept himself neat and tidy. He lived in a two up two down crumbling end terrace without running water, indoor toilet, radio, telephone, gas or electricity. Nothing. No lighting except for candles, no cooking stove and the only heating and cooking was from an open fireplace with a trivet suspended over the fire; from the trivet could be hung a kettle or a pot.

One sunny morning (it must have been in 1946 because I remember thinking Patsy is 10 times my age, meaning that Patsy was 70 and I was 7) Patsy and I were leaning on the sea wall chatting about the weather and the news of the village as one did, when Patsy said slowly and gently, "Stephen, I will die a happy man." Curious, I asked him why. His reply came, "I am seventy years old today. I will die a happy man. I have £30 saved above in the shop with your father. He has promised me that he will see that I get a proper funeral with a proper coffin and a hearse – no pauper's grave for me. Until that time comes, I can live comfortably on my state pension which gives me 10 shillings and sixpence (about *€0.60 or £0.52 in today's money*) a week."

I found this interesting at the time but in today's mad world of insatiable consumerism I find it reverberates in my brain.

CHAPTER XIII

GERRY BAKER AND FUNERALS

Having three hugely energetic sons so close in age must have meant a lot of work and worry for my Mother. She herself was a woman of enormous energy. She helped Father in the business at busy times of the week. She managed the Union Hall shop when he went to the Leap shop four afternoons a week or when he was away on meetings of the Synod or other Church work. She cooked superbly to satisfy Father's love of good food. She not only made all the marmalade and jams we required for the family but huge amounts extra for sale in the shop. Mother baked almost every day - bread, cakes and scones during the year and festive cakes and puddings for special occasions and holidays. She preserved all the usual suspects: raspberries, blackcurrants, gooseberries, strawberries, crab apples and plums. Her blackberry and apple pie was historic.

Mother made our own butter. Father used a hand operated separating machine to get cream when we had surplus milk from our small dairy herd, to which Mother then added salt and hand churned it into butter. The butter milk did not go to waste either because that was used in the baking of her traditional bread.

She even made her own soap and candles during the years of rationing caused by the war.

She hand knitted garments for all the family, producing countless gloves, socks, sweaters, cardigans, scarves (I can still feel the ache in my arms whilst I held open the hanks of wool to enable her to rewind it into balls). She crocheted tablecloths and placemats not only for our family but also to give as presents.

With three young boys in the house, Mother was constantly patching and mending clothes. On one occasion I protested that she had gone too far. Fed up patching the seats of our trousers, she hit on the great wheeze of putting the patch on when the trousers were new and then merely removing the patch when we inevitably wore holes in it. This of course meant that we never had pristine trousers - either they were new and patched or they were without a patch but somewhat worn.

What I find incredible was that Mother was doing all of the above without electricity. So no refrigerator, no freezer, no electric cooker. Kitchen stirrers and beaters were of the hand operated variety only. Her Jones sewing machine was driven by a foot treadle.

In my early memories we always had a maid to help Mother with these tasks. The maid was usually taken on as a 15 year old and taught by Mother all the key skills in which she required help. They usually left at about 20, either to get married or emigrate to get more money. One of their key tasks was to take us kids for a walk after lunch to get us out of the way whilst Mother had a much deserved short siesta.

In 1947 petrol rationing ended and a new era opened up for the village. Funerals were and are hugely important in Irish life. In my view a good funeral can add greatly to the cohesion of society. As well as fostering good neighbourliness, such social gatherings can be a cause of jealousy and rivalry. A family's status was judged on the size of the attendance at their funerals and the importance of the people attending. As a pillar of the community, Father's attendance helped to establish the importance of the dead man.

From Father's point of view it was good business because it made his customers and potential customers even better disposed to trading with him. However attending so many funerals was hugely time consuming.

There were no private cars at all allowed during the war years of 1939 to 1945. Once private motor cars were again on the road after World War Two, a key status symbol was the number of motor cars at a funeral. I have heard many conversations such as "Was it a big funeral?" and the reply, "Yes, there were 15 cars at it."

Father then had a brain wave. He could get his customers goodwill and save time. He would send Gerry Baker (full name Jeremiah O' Donovan) in our car to the funeral and get the deceased person's families approval for enhancing their funeral whilst he himself could get on with his business. Gerry worked in the shop and also acted as Fathers boatman when we went fishing. Amongst his many other duties was looking after us children when possible. Suffice it to say for now that we children loved, trusted and took huge advantage of Gerry's endless patience and good nature. He adored us, spoiled us, taught us and did his considerable best to keep us out of danger.

Then Mother too had a brainwave. The car had to go to the funeral anyway. Why not pack us three children in the back of the car where we could not do much damage and get us out of the way for several hours? This suited all concerned. Mother had peace of mind. Gerry could look after his beloved 'ladeens' as he described us. We had a very indulgent carer, we had the sweets with which we were bribed to behave ourselves and we were free from Mother's vigilance.

It was the custom after a death to lay the corpse in the parlour (sitting room). A "wake" was held which consisted of people calling in to pay their respects to the family, view the corpse and be given large amounts of whiskey and food. Poteen* was often on offer. After a day or so the corpse was taken to the church where it lay overnight. I cannot say in any more detail what was involved because we children were never allowed to participate. The part we were involved in took place the next day. Mourners gathered at the church and filed past the coffin to view the deceased again before the lid was finally screwed down. We children were not supposed to do the filing past bit but we usually managed a quick peep. Thus

---

*Poteen (potin in the Irish spelling) is an alcohol distilled illegally from potatoes or grain, often in remote boggy areas so as not to arouse suspicion of the law with its potent smell. I remember first trying Poteen at the age of 14.

by the time I was 10, I must have seen a couple of hundred dead bodies. I cannot recall feeling either squeamish or apprehensive – more an attitude of acceptance and mild curiosity.

Afterwards we got back into the car scrummaging and wrestling all the way to the graveyard. We then accompanied the mourners to the grave and exchanged greetings and courtesies with the grown-ups. The coffin was lowered into the grave and the funeral mass was said. The grave was filled with earth. We then went home to have our afternoon tea, tired and happy after another eventful day.

CHAPTER XIV

THE REVENGE OF A WRONGED UNION HALL MAN

One of my Father's friends was the well known solicitor Willie Kingston. A bachelor, Willie wrote a detailed autobiography / diary. I have a copy. as has Terry Kearney at the excellent Heritage Museum in Skibbereen. Willie swore that he was present at Skibbereen District Court in the 1920s when the following took place:

A man from the Union Hall locality had been charged with poaching. The judges were not the full time judges we usually have nowadays but were magistrates, that is men of some local prominence who volunteered to act as judges. It was rumoured that some or perhaps all of the magistrates were the illegitimate offspring of Colonel Spaight of Union Hall. The chap protested his innocence at some length in the face of overwhelming evidence to the contrary. Despite his protests the magistrates found the Union Hall man guilty.

The chap was angered by what he considered to be an injustice inflicted on him by people who were not themselves of total moral rectitude. He vented his annoyance by proclaiming this little ditty:

"Gentlemen of the Bench before I depart
Let me say a few words that come straight from my heart.
Though innocent I am, it is guilty I'm found
By ye that were made against walls or on ground.
Though your mothers had men, they never were wed
And ye convicted a man who was made in a bed.
………..Anyway you're a pack of bastards"

When reciting this type of song it is usual to be very strong and quite slow in delivering all except the last line. The last line is said quickly, almost gabbled. Try it and see if it works for you.

CHAPTER XV

DAVID AND THE FORGE

Nowadays the area immediately opposite our family house and shop is an open air store belonging to Noel Fuller, my nephew and Godson, which is a parking area for his customers. In my childhood this space occupied by the store was a forge and the area occupied by the car park was one single storey cabin and three two storey derelict terraced houses. The derelict houses were one of the many interesting places in which we could play. In our imagination these houses became castles to defend, army barracks in which to plan the defeat of the enemy, football pitches, a shooting range for our bows and arrows. However the play area was only a secondary attraction compared to David's forge.

The forge consisted of a massive open fire of coal and coke which all day long emitted an eerie red light accompanied by sulphurous fumes. The fire was kept at maximum heat by a gigantic bellows.

David made many pieces of farm and domestic equipment from the iron which he bought in our shop. He made such things as gates, water tanks, fire fenders, metallic stools and so on. But the major part of his earnings came from creating horseshoes and applying them to the horses.

The forge was a very exciting place for a small boy to be, banging, crashing; spurts of steam, lurid lighting, and weird smells from the annealing process but particularly from the horses 'toenail' as David cut and filed it. What added to my joy and wonder was the feeling of importance when David actually allowed me to pump the bellows.

I was also intrigued by the half-naked sweating David as he toiled in the heat and murk to shoe the horses. Even at that age I knew that he was afraid of some of the horses and I watched, half in frightened expectation, and it must be said, a fair amount of admiration.

I spent so much time at the forge that it became almost routine. It seemed to me it was part of every small boy's life that they would go across the road to the forge.

Fast forward to 21st July 1969 when I am a married man living with my wife and three delightful daughters in Dundalk, Southern Ireland. All week the children have been looking forward to a television programme which has its main excitement a horse being shoed. Julie was 6½, Sarah 4 and Vanessa 2½. They were outraged when I insisted that they change the television channel to watch something that I said was so momentous that they would remember it all their lives. I have checked with them recently and they have no memory of it whatsoever.

The significance of the date is that the 21st July 1969 was the day that Neil Armstrong and Buzz Aldrin made the first successful man on the moon walk.

To me the man on the moon walk was highly exciting and the horse being shoed merely routine. To my children men walked on the moon every day in their television cartoons. The shoeing of the horse was a much more exciting event.

CHAPTER XVI

THE RICHARD AND THE CANARY ISLANDERS

Noel Fuller has on display in Union Hall a lovely model of a sailing coastal vessel.

The Richard was a commercial cargo boat owned by Great Grandmother Fuller's oldest uncle Richard. My father Noel Stephen told me this story a number of times when I was a small boy but we never talked about it in my adult years, so I do not have all the details.

At the time of the story Anne Moxley, who later married Thomas Fuller, was working in her uncle's grocery shop. Richard Moxley, her other uncle, made his living using the boat to transport goods up and down the Irish coast with occasional trips to Great Britain. The Richard was his pride and joy. Looking at the model one can see why. Glorious and elegant are two words which come to mind. This beauty is despite my mother replacing the sails and rigging sometime in the 1950s. I remember her telling me that she had simplified things because "they were so complicated and, besides, no one will know". Every time I see the model, I regret hugely her shortcut. Hopefully someday Noel will have the model Richard rerigged and resailed.

Richard Moxley had traded his way up a succession of ever bigger boats and the Richard was the pinnacle of his achievement so he called her after himself.

One day in the 1840s a battered little fishing boat came into the harbour. The boat was a mess and so were the crew. They told of fierce storms which had blown them off course and which prevented them from getting back to their home port in the Canary Islands. They had completely run out of food and had no local currency. The locals were, as always, very hospitable and looked after the bedraggled strangers. Anne Moxley gave them provisions from the shop, saying that they could send her the money when they got home.

Early the following morning, somebody rushed to Richard Moxley's house to tell him the Richard was leaving the harbour. They thought that the Canary Islanders had taken her and left their own little boat behind. Richard Moxley jumped on his horse to ride to the harbour to see that the Richard was indeed no longer there. He rode the horse around the coast to the cliffs east of Glandore to it disappearing over the horizon. This was the last he saw of his beloved boat.

Despite his best efforts no trace of the Richard was ever found.

Stanley, Stephen, and Stuart

CHAPTER XVII

<u>FISHING</u>

One of my greatest pleasures is sea fishing. The feel of the wind borne sea salt on my lips is very special. The wind can be so soothing, so gentle. Off the South West coast of Ireland that balmy fresh feeling is not emulated in any of the other coastal waters I have experienced. It seems to me to denote bliss. Perhaps it is just me. Perhaps I credit that wind with the peace and contentment which going to sea with my Father, brothers and our boatman Gerry Baker generated. Whatever the reason it really felt so good. As the saying goes, 'It warms the cockles of your heart'.

That coast in which Union Hall sits must be one of the most attractive in the whole wide world. I have travelled and fished off many coasts but I have never seen anything more beautiful than that stretch of coast between the Fastnet lighthouse to the West and the Old Head of Kinsale lighthouse to the East. Heavily indented into many harbours. Many small islands and islets. Beauty at all times but especially at sunset. The setting sun seems to emphasise even more the glory of the scenery. The colours are divine.

We enjoyed fishing so much we quite often went to sea when more sensible people stayed ashore. The wind and waves were exhilarating, dangerous even. On the days when the wind was very strong the waves could be as much as 2 metres high. At the crest of a wave the wind howled and then the boat would slip into the trough; there one could not feel the wind but neither could one see the land – exciting for me but dreadful for those liable to sea sickness. I early on learnt to stay upwind of those unfortunates. A capful of vomit is something to be avoided.

Such trips stimulated one's appetite enormously. Often we would land in a sheltered cove on one of the islands. Then with great anticipation we would open the boxes into which Mother had packed the food. Even now I can smell the home baked wholemeal bread, the roast chicken, and see the vivid colours: the green of the lettuce, the red of the tomatoes, the radishes with that unique red and hear the crunch of the raw celery.

I have inherited Father's aversion to tea from a vacuum flask, and so we would have to wait for the water to heat on a Primus* stove.

On one occasion Father, Gerry, 9 year old me, and Billy Colthurst landed on Cape Clear Island to picnic. Cape Clear, with a population of about 100 and 8 miles off the coast near Baltimore, is one of Carberry's Hundred Isles. It is a lovely island among many lovely islands. Officially Cape Clear was and is a Gaeltacht - which means that most people can speak both Irish and English. The Government in its desire to promote the Irish language gave (and I think still gives) many sizeable grants to people who speak Irish and remain in the Gaeltacht. Much to our despair we could not light the Primus because the jet was blocked. To unblock a Primus jet a special needle is required and we did not have one. Gerry and I set off to find somebody from whom we could buy, beg or borrow a Primus needle. Billy Colthurst decided he would come with us for the exercise.

Billy was a curate in the North of Ireland and son of our local

---

* For those of you who have not heard of a Primus, here is a summary of what Wikipedia says: *The Primus stove was the first pressurized kerosene oil stove. The burner was rather like a blowtorch which focussed the heat on to the cooking pot or kettle. The fuel tank was in the base. A steel top ring on which to set a pot was held over the burner by three support legs.*

Church of Ireland rector. He did not have suitable fishing clothes so chose to wear an old suit - too shabby for a curate in a prim and proper North of Ireland parish, but far too good for a chap fishing off a small island off South-West Cork. Obviously, Billy did not wear his clerical collar but nevertheless he looked decidedly posh.

After some time we were delighted to encounter a lady. Clearly a local (it was possible to tell from a persons' clothes, hair style even stance even before they spoke). Gerry asked her if she would help us to find a primus needle, but none of us understood her lengthy reply in Irish. Our need was great so Gerry persevered. No joy. Eventually the exasperated lady managed to say "No speaka da Inglis".

Billy, by now totally fed up, wandered off to see if he could find somebody to help. Gerry kept going and the woman kept up this babble we could not understand. Eventually the kindly Gerry, exasperated, said: "Jaysus Missus, why won't you talk to us?" after checking to see that Billy in his fine suit was out of earshot, the woman said in very clear English: "I'm not going to speak English in front of one of them government men. They can take away your Gaeltacht grant, you know."

***

On a different occasion we landed on yet another of Carberry's Hundred Islands. In a sheltered spot were the remains of a single storey stone built cottage, roof long gone. I asked Father why the cottage had been left empty. He told this tale.

The cottage had been lived in by a hard working thrifty family up until the mid-1920s. Father knew this family very well; they were highly respected and good customers of his shop. Despite being good fishermen, prices for fish were low so far from the big towns. The family did their best to make a living from the 40-50 acres of land, which had really poor soil and was plagued by the sea spray and the winds. But times were hard.

Their land however had one great potential earner. The strand (beach) was the recipient of all things on the surface of the sea. During the First World War all sorts of debris from ships sunk at sea was washed up on to their and the surrounding beaches. Even in peacetime many ships had deck cargo which was often blown overboard in bad weather.

This marine debris is called flotsam and jetsam. The technical distinction between flotsam and jetsam and the ownership of them can be legally quite difficult, made even more complex by whether they were found above or below the high-water mark. In any case the legal ownership is divided in different complicated ways between the original owner, the Government and the finder.

The cottagers were in the ideal place to find this marine debris. Either it was washed up on one of the several beaches of the island or they found it floating. The family were baffled by all of these complicated rules and regulations – so they arrived at a simple solution: They would not tell anyone.

Not wanting to put the Custom Officers or the Coastguards to any trouble they decided to stow their finds away safely. The most valuable things they hid in the thatched roof. The rest they sold off cheaply, throwing items with no value back to the sea.

A few years after the war ended the family did a rough calculation of the value of the hoard in the thatch. Reckoning it was worth more than the value of the little cottage with its outbuildings and small farm, they decided to keep it stashed 'for a rainy day' as they did not need the money immediately.

Then one dreadful night the thatched roof caught fire. In the blaze they lost virtually everything that they had so carefully stored. No insurance. Nothing they could do. Can you imagine their agony? Absolutely no one to blame but themselves. Devastated, without the will to even repair the little cottage, the family moved to the mainland.

***

One tranquil autumn evening Father and I went out fishing alone. My brothers were not there because they had gone back to school whilst I had the longer University summer vacation. We had a pleasant evening's fishing. Nothing record breaking in the size of the catch. Nevertheless a decent haul. Pleasant time. Gentle inconsequential chatting with intervals of comfortable silences.

As we entered the inner harbour close to the small islet called Eve, Father said quietly "look to your left". There was a very long fish on the surface about 7 or 8 metres away keeping pace with the boat: a basking shark.

The shark unperturbed was keeping one lazy eye on us. Whereas we, particularly me, were bursting with excitement.

Father slowed the engine to allow us to see even more of the giant. A triangular fin showed above the water. The body was relatively slim. Two grey green fins or wings could be seen just below the surface. A vast mouth was open apparently to allow the shark to filter the tiny plankton from the seawater.

After a while I got a little bored and, to Father's unspoken disapproval poked the shark with an oar. No reaction whatsoever.

As we entered the harbour further the shark idly slipped away. Somehow I felt a perfect end to a perfect evening. Just Father and I. And then that glorious creature.

CHAPTER XVIII

FARMING

Farming as a means of earning a living has never interested me. Why? It is not the long hours. I have almost always worked long hours. I certainly would prefer not to have to put up with the cold rain driving down the back of my neck but I have tolerated that when fishing or playing outdoor sports in all weather. Some of the smells in farming are truly glorious, but have you ever smelled a pig sty?

I have never wanted to farm because of the uncertainty in farming. My psyche desires predictability and farming could never be sufficiently certain. The weather, commodity prices, government interference just make farming too much of a lottery for me. I need the control which commerce and industry can give. My chosen gamble has always been: "Heads I win and tails I don't lose."

Such advanced economic thinking played no part in the thinking of the young Stephen. I loved the open air, the climbing of hay stacks, the sheer adventure that was available. We small boys had a wonderful time on the 30 acres which Father had as one of his many interests. Whilst small it was very productive. The farm was run using the latest ideas of that time. It helped that the soil was excellent and well drained. Father was one of the first to use the black and white Friesian cattle for his small milking herd.

When I was a small boy we always had at least one horse. When the grass grew long enough to make hay, it was the horse that pulled the cutting machine. When the cut grass became hay under the rays of the sun, it was the horse that pulled the wheeled rake which gathered the hay into piles. When the hay needed to be transported to the barn it was the horse that pulled the cart. When I wanted to become my comic book hero Roy Rogers it was the horse who had the role of Silver, Roy Rogers' steed, young me sat atop exclaiming Roy Rogers' catchphrase as he embarked on another brave venture, Heigh Ho, Silver!

We small boys helped with those tasks. We used the hand rakes to gather the mown hay into haycocks in preparation for the hay being transported to the barn. When the hay was being stowed in the barn it was our job to jump on it so it packed down and more hay could be stowed. We also scattered the coarse salt in the hay to "sweeten" it. Certainly it did have a strong sweet smell. It was very hot in the barn, especially when the hay got to be close to the roof. Hard work but fun also.

When we got older, say 7 or 8, we drove the cows in from the fields so that they could be milked. Brother Stuart even mastered the art of hand milking the cows, as a child I was so envious that I just could not do it (although when we became teenagers home from boarding school I was very pleased that I was so inept whereas Stuart as a master milker was often asked to do it).

As we drove the cows through the street I was embarrassed because they chose to drop their cow dung wherever they went. However I soon realized that the people whose houses the cows passed did not mind at all. They came out of the houses with pans to gather up the cow dung for their back gardens and vegetable gardens. I must say that the tomatoes fertilized by our cows were the tastiest I have ever had. I recall especially a lady who had a barrel of water to which was added cow dung twice a day. The resultant fertilizer was very effective.

When I was about 5 Mother persuaded Father that the garden at the back of our house was not large enough or fertile enough for her to grow the quantity and type of fruit and vegetables she wanted, so he gave her half an acre of farmland where the farm abutted onto the back of the yard. I think he did not realise that this meant he also provided her with men from the business to do the necessary heavy work.

It was worth it though as Mother grew wonderful fresh fruit and vegetables earned considerable money by selling the surplus in the shops.

Mother also enlisted her sons. Unfortunately she used us only as cheap labour. We did not get any training in gardening which would have been so useful in later life. So we hoed, we pruned, we picked raspberries, black and white currants, we erected supports for peas and beans and sweetpeas. We watered. We fetched and carried. But no master class in growing fruit and vegetables. She was a wonderful Mum in most other ways, so maybe she thought that it was woman's work and not for men.

One benefit however did come from the gardening. I got to fire Father's shotgun. At the age of 11, Mother came to me one day and said "Your Father never has the time to shoot the pigeons and other birds that are the scourge of my garden. Go and get his 12 bore shotgun".

I did not need telling twice.

I had always watched him intently when Father took us out rough shooting. I really *really* wanted to use that gun. I knew exactly what to do. Oh joy, here was Mum asking me to use Father's gun.

One of my tasks for many years after that was to shoot any birds who tried to invade Mother's garden. It did not involve killing many birds. I just shot one of each species and then hung them up which effectively scared the others off.

It did not occur to my Mother or me to think that we might have been doing anything wrong or even unkind. As a farmer's daughter she saw it as the right and proper thing to do to kill these birds who were eating her crops. At that age I had no reason to question her belief. Even now when I have read opposing views I am satisfied that we were doing the right thing. One could also question my Father's duties of responsibility for an 11 year old me being allowed to use a shotgun in the vicinity of a village. Again I am satisfied that he did the right thing. He had always taught us boys about the protocols of safe shooting. He had suffered the loss of an eye as a young man and was very aware of the dangers of misusing a shotgun.

Indeed one can question why my parents and their contemporaries allowed children to work. My brothers and I worked both in the business and on the farm. I believe that today it would be considered illegal. The reality is that we boys enjoyed doing those tasks. We were never forced to do anything. We saw it as a privilege. We got praise and encouragement. We had the companionship of being with the people we loved. We loved not only my parents but also the employees in the business and on the farm. Also I think that we had a quiet pride that we were doing grown up things and helping the family enterprise. In my opinion it was much preferable to the electronic games and social media that takes up the time of today's young people. Indeed all my children worked in the factory when on holiday from boarding school and they tell me they enjoyed it.

Martha and Noel Fuller.
Below with their grandchildren Mark, Julie,
Sarah, Janice, Vanessa, Ann, Keith and Hazel.

PART TWO

1947 – 1961

EDUCATION

CHAPTER XIX

IS CUMA LIOM

From a very early age I have always been intrigued by the motivation behind one's behaviour, particularly my own.

For instance when I went to Miss Swanton's school I really didn't wish to go at all. I could not see why I should leave my childhood haven of Union Hall, with all its nooks and crannies, to be incarcerated in a stuffy room with a lady for whom I had no respect. I certainly was not interested in anything she had to say. Consequently, I reached my 7th birthday effectively unable to read. Then I discovered comics and I was so fascinated that within a short space of time I could read all of them particularly my beloved Eagle. I found bookcases full of books left over from my father's childhood. One which particularly caught my imagination was

Treasure Island by Robert Louis Stevenson. This newfound fascination meant that within a year I was a very accomplished reader.

After leaving Miss Swanton's school for Brandon Grammar school my attitude to formal education changed very little. I still had no respect for teachers and could see no point in their lessons. My refusal to complete any homework whatsoever led to my being sent to the Headmaster for caning.

The Headmaster Ivan McCutcheon, a man for whom I soon had a very high regard and great affection, wielded the cane in such a gentle fashion that it was of no deterrent to me whatsoever. However, one had to queue at the end of the school day for the punishment and this wasted a lot of valuable time that could be spent on the games fields. I soon decided it was better to at least do something to stop this waste of time and I paid token attention to the teachers and to my homework.

To my amazement I began to find that what the teachers had to say was actually interesting. To my surprise and to the surprise of many around me I was put up not one class but two classes. This move was certainly not justified either by my age or by my pathetic scholastic achievements. In the new form I confirmed my growing interest in learning and consequently finished the year near the top of the form. So what made the difference? The difference was not my ability but my motivation.

Certainly I must pay tribute to Ivan McCutcheon and his staff for spotting that this rebellious pugnacious red haired brat had in fact a brain underneath the façade and that the way to tackle it was to give him more and more work. This is a lesson which I have followed throughout my life, if I find an idle colleague I give them even more work and expect even more from then. I have found it almost always works.

I was not however so accomplished in all school subjects. My results in Irish were abysmal. The problem was that I could not find any stories in Irish that rivalled the sorts of stories I enjoyed in English. In the Irish stories we were taught there were no heroes, no dashing pilots, no interplanetary travel and no humour, which I found in English books and comics. In Irish, I had Peig, which was just the gloomy story of an old woman with a life that had no relevance to us youngsters. And later on O Peann an Piarsaig by Padraig Pearse, which again was nothing compared to the adventures I found in English literature. Despite Irish being taught by the wonderful Miss Irene Simpson, I just could not get motivated to get the interest aroused, which I have always needed to do something well. This is highlighted by the fact Miss Simpson also taught Latin and I did well in that. Again Vergil, Caesar and Cicero grabbed my imagination.

One anecdote from those school days learning Irish still brings a smile to my lips: aged about 13 I was sitting in an Irish class when an inspection** was announced.

As usual I was sitting next to my great friend Peter Anderson. The inspector asked a question to the front row and nobody could answer it, so he went through the whole form asking the same question to each person with no result. When it came to Peter's turn Peter had no answer to give out loud but I did hear him mutter, "N*il fios agam agus is Cuma liom"*. I heard this and wondered why Peter didn't at least say it out loud because it would be some answer even if it was the wrong answer. So when it came to my

---

*To my horror my Grandchildren in Kerry had their entire schooling in Irish - imagine having to learn English through Irish.

**The Department for Education used to send inspectors to check up on the way Irish was being taught in all schools. If the school did not achieve satisfactory standards then the government grant to that school was taken away. Another bit of evidence of the draconian attitude display

turn I said brightly out loud: "N*il fios agam agus is Cuma liom"*. The inspector looked astonished, paused a moment and then said in English: "Boy if you had known what you were saying you would never have said it."

Curiosity aroused, I looked up the meaning, which is: "I don't know and I don't care!"

CHAPTER XX

UNIVERSITY

From the age when one starts to properly think about such things I assumed* that I would go to University. I also knew that I would go to Trinity more properly known as Trinity College Dublin, Dublin University - TCD for short. I did not concern myself about such things as Entrance Examinations or Fees. I just knew.

This was partly the result of W. Ivan McCutcheon's tie.

Mr. McCutcheon, known as Mac to both his pupils and staff was the headmaster at Bandon Grammar School. A Trinity graduate

---

*By the way, do you know the joke?

Question: What happens when you ASSUME? Answer: It makes an ASS of U and ME

Mac loved to tell stories about his time at University, and as and of the 'Hist' – Dublin University's Historical Society. He was my role model in a number of ways and he inspired me to want to go there.

Ivan McCutcheon's contemporary in the Hist was RB McDowell, known to many as RB. RB, although exceedingly clever, could not be relied upon to dress himself properly and had to be helped into the White Tie and gown which the officers of the Hist were required to wear. In my days at Trinity RB was the Junior Dean. On one occasion, when invigilating an exam, RB threw one of my fellow students out of the exam hall for "not being academically dressed" (the student in question had thrown his black exam gown over his shoulder in a most pathetic manner). Fed up, the young man sat on the steps of the Exam Hall smoking a cigarette. RB, having been relieved of his invigilator duties, saw him smoking, and having quite forgotten that he had thrown the chap out, ignored all protests and fined him for "smoking whilst wearing academic dress".

***

Quite early on in my life, I decided that I would like a career that would enable me to travel the world. Civil Engineering seemed to me to be a job that would allow me to earn a decent salary, do interesting work, and see all sorts of places around the world. To my mind, Civil Engineering would entail building bridges and roads in exotic places; I had visions of being in charge of projects such as building bridges across the Zambezi River in Central Africa.

I passed the necessary examinations quite easily and started Trinity University in October 1957. To my horror I soon found that the School of Engineering was not the exciting place I had imagined. On the contrary, the boring lessons were delivered by men* who had got into something of a rut a long time ago. Luckily I was very good at both English and Mathematics, the two key subjects in Engineering. Accordingly, I did not have to do much work to keep up with my studies.

One of my lecturers who was an exception to the 'stuffy old man' rule, was 'Pip' Graham. I call him Pip because I never heard him called anything else, I do not know if this was his full name. Pip stimulated us with his excellent knowledge of his subject and his delight in teaching us. He was a cheerful man and always full of fun. His apparently light hearted approach to his subject and to life

---

*All of the Engineering staff and students were male in those days.

did not hinder in any way his brilliance as a teacher and guide.

At that time the President of the Republic of Ireland was Eamonn de Valera. A tall august figure almost always dressed mostly in black, de Valera was not known for his sense of humour. Now in his eighties he indulged himself in his hobbies, one of which was Dublin University Mathematical Society. He would turn up without fanfare attended by just a driver and one bodyguard both from the Garda Special Branch. Very straight backed, the President moved slowly and solemnly.

The Mathematics Society often held its evening meetings in a room in the Museum Building. The Museum building is one of the delights of Trinity. Finished in 1857 it is a wonderful palazzo style building inspired by the Byzantine architecture of Venice. I particularly like the interior; finished in a variety of stone mostly from Irish quarries, it had glorious coloured marbles. The sweeping wide stairways with their handrail also in marble were very impressive. I say handrail but they were really about half a metre wide.

One evening before the Maths Society meeting Pip was bored waiting for proceedings to begin. So, dressed in his academic clothing, he decided to slide down the handrail which he did very successfully but he fell off at the end and landed in a heap at de Valera's feet. Pip looked up smiling and said "I've always wanted to do that." The President of Ireland, looking down from his great height, said with a hint of a smile: "Good evening, Pip".

***

Sport was my main activity at Trinity. I was also a member of the two principal debating societies, The Historical Society and the Philosophical Society. Accordingly, I can claim that my interests did include some more civilized pastimes than chasing people and balls around the landscape. I did take part in debates on topics that I found really interesting, but why join both societies when they were really competitors? The answer; they each had a billiard room and sometimes it was easier to get a table in one than the other.

Hockey was my favourite sport. I enjoyed it at both my boarding schools Bandon Grammar School and Mountjoy School Dublin. I had been sufficiently proficient to play for Munster Schools in the interprovincial tournament whilst at Bandon and then for Leinster Schools whilst at Mountjoy. This gave me a head start when I entered Trinity and I got my Colours playing for the University.

One of my hockey club members was Andrew Bonar-Law. Grandson of a prime minister he may have been but respecter of rules and regulations he was not.

At that time motorists had to place a disc on the car windscreen to show that the Road Tax had been paid. Andrew saved money by displaying a Guinness label where other people displayed a tax disc. On one occasion Andrew parked his Triumph Mayflower with a Guinness label where the tax disc should be, directly outside the Garda police station nearly opposite the Back Gate entrance into the University grounds.

Returning to his car, Andrew spotted a Garda loitering close to the Triumph Mayflower. He rushed back into the Trinity coffee shop to recruit help. A number of us hatched a plan, here is what happened: At a pedestrian crossing further up Pearse Street a chap crossing the road was run into by a cyclist. There was much uproar and cries from the injured parties made worse by onlookers bemoaning their fate, some blaming the pedestrian and some the cyclist. The Garda, distracted by all the fuss, went to sort things out. Whereupon Andrew jumped into his car and reversed at high speed through Back Gate. The Garda rushed to try to stop Andrew but then had to halt at back Gate because he could not enter Trinity without specific permission. In disgust the Garda went to sort out the accident and the injured parties but they had all vanished.

***

Rowing was another sport which I enjoyed during my time at Trinity, although it was not as important to me as hockey and rugby. I rowed for the Engineering School at the Trinity regatta. Chris Mallagh was the cox because he was the lightest of our friends. Plev Ellis was the stroke because entering the Regatta was his idea. Ernie Boyle was in because he was very fit and strong.

George Hallowes was in because he was an all round nice fellow. I was in because I was the only one who had done any significant amount of rowing, although all my previous rowing had been done on craft with fixed seats whereas on the river we were using a shell with sliding seats. I was on the bow oar to make up for Mallagh's steering deficiencies. I believe that we cannot have been the worst because we scored two bumps.

I have always considered that my main activity at Trinity was talking and listening. One grew up in an atmosphere of so many, usually intelligent, people with so many ideas and opinions. Seemingly endless discussions through the night often ended without conclusion. But one gained the ability to come to think reasonably clearly. I came to value this ability to think my way through situations and to know what I wanted.

Stephen in Trinity College Dublin hockey team
(top row, second to left)

PART THREE

1961 - 2019

FAMILY

Stephen and Geraldine on their wedding day

CHAPTER XXI

THE START OF MARRIED LIFE

Geraldine and I were married in 1962 in Dublin. I had met her at the Rathmines Tennis Club. It was all very pleasant and light hearted until we realised that I was soon to graduate and move into the "great wide world" and the probability was that we might never see one another again, and so we married. It was a wonderful day and there is a photo album to show it.

However, we were broke.

We had saved for a honeymoon in Switzerland but six weeks before we were due to go the Travel Agency announced that they were closing and they had not actually booked our holiday. Furthermore they could not repay us. I went to see the lady who ran it with her useless husband and 'persuaded' them to return our money. I bought a brand new minivan, taxed and insured for £380. Geraldine arranged a two week tour of B&Bs in Scotland – Edinburgh, Inverness, Loch Lomond, and Fort William. Bliss.

At the end of the honeymoon on the way to Somerset we stopped at a lay-by near Lancaster to review the situation. I had driven 150 miles already and Geraldine did not have a driving license. It was evening time. We were 250 miles from Plymouth with only 1 shilling and 10 pence in cash and a cheque for £5.

Friends of Geraldine's Mother owned a hotel in Lancaster where we may have been able to cash the cheque. However our pride prevented us from going there to cash the cheque for fear they would think we were trying to scrounge a bed for the night.

Stubbornly, we spent the money on some currant buns for dinner and tried sleeping in the minivan overnight. So cold. By 7 in the morning we gave in and drove to the hotel. As predicted they were overwhelmingly kind, they insisted on giving us a huge breakfast and cashed the cheque. Well fed and with money in our pockets we cruised back to Plymouth.

Thus we started married life – no money to spare but a forerunner to a really truly enjoyable life.

CHAPTER XXII

<u>THE GIRLS</u>

Julie was born January 12, 1963. When Geraldine was 34 weeks pregnant with our first child she had to go into hospital in Plymouth, Devon with dangerously high blood pressure. Our tiny one bedroom flat, without any help, was just no place for a first time Mother suffering from a dangerous condition.

After leaving Geraldine at the hospital I was extremely worried. To distract myself, I visited our friends Peter and Belinda Roberts. We opened and finished a bottle of cheap brandy they had brought back from holiday.

Waking the next morning with a terrible headache I rushed to the nearby phone box. To my shock, when I enquired to the Nurse how Geraldine was, she replied, "Your wife and baby daughter are both doing very well."

We were woefully underprepared (having not expected Julie to arrive for another six weeks). We had no cot, no pram, no cloth nappies, nothing prepared.

Our pride would not let us entertain the idea of asking for an advance from my employer nor ask for a loan from our parents.

The solution was to borrow £20 from the Bank. The Bank Manager would agree to give me the loan only after I agreed to take out an insurance policy (on which I am sure he earned a large commission). This loan allowed us to buy a multi-function pram/carry and sleeping cot for £16. The remaining £4 was spent very carefully.

It took some time to organise that. So when Mum and baby came home after a few days in hospital the necessary things were not all in place. Accordingly the wonderful baby spent her first three nights at home sleeping in the long drawer at the bottom of our old-fashioned wardrobe.

***

Sarah was born July 9, 1965. This was a complete contrast to the drama and anxieties of Julie's birth. The local GP, a wonderful man whose name I forget, waged war on the local hospital because he considered it awful. He and his so efficient midwife decreed that the baby would be born at home.

Thus on the 9th July everyone was gathered in our huge main bedroom waiting for the main event. We were all relaxed and happy. Occasionally I popped into the adjacent living room to have a cigarette. After a very little fuss Sarah's head, adorned with a full head of black hair, emerged slowly and quietly into the world. When all was tidied up and the excitement died down I said one of the silliest things: "I don't know what all the fuss about childbirth is. I have been hurt a lot more on the rugby field!"

Some weeks later Geraldine said to me: "We have to register the baby's birth. Go into Shepton Mallet to the Registrar at this address. Remember to spell the names correctly S-A-R-A-H J-O-A-N-N. Joann is one word and there is no E. I wish to have it this way because my Mum's name is Joan and my own second name is Ann." I duly trotted off to the Shepton Mallet Registrar. She turned out to resemble a rather fierce dragon and be much older than my 25 years. She snapped "Date of Birth?" Horror struck and, intimidated, I just could not remember the exact date. So the Dragon made me phone Geraldine to get the date – I felt so diminished.

When asked for the names I was triumphant and said boldly "Sarah Joann and it must be spelled exactly like that". She glared at me and snorted "Don't be silly young man, there is no such spelling as Joann." She made me ring Geraldine again just to confirm that it was really Joann.

***

Vanessa Jane was born February 28 1967. Vanessa's birth was even more gentle and non-eventful than Sarah's. This time I made no reference to rugby but congratulated all and sundry on how well things had been done.

By now we owned our own house. A decent sized semi with four bedrooms and large gardens front and rear. 147 Ard Easmuinn, Dundalk. Granny Haynes was delighted to have Julie and Sarah for the few weeks before and after the due date. Lovely Dr. Murphy, the midwife and Mrs. O'Reilly the daily had everything well organised and under control. A little before midnight Vanessa Jane arrived with very little fuss.

Although this birth was longer than with Sarah it was even more peaceful, without much strain and even more good humoured. In between visits to the bedroom Dr.Murphy and I, with Geraldine and the midwife's permission, retired to the kitchen to discuss politics whilst smoking.

I was present at both Sarah and Nessa's births. Both Geraldine and I found that the 'Dad being present at birth experience' pleasant and worthwhile. It helped to bond Geraldine and I even closer.

Vanessa was the chosen name because Geraldine particularly liked it. Jane because we thought we would give each of the children a fancy name and a simple one if that was what the child wanted for herself in later life.

Vanessa was spoilt rotten by her two older sisters. So much so that we realised when Vanessa was almost two years old that she did not/could not talk with us. Her sisters looked after and communicated with her so effectively that they would say "she wants this" or "she doesn't like that" or whatever. Vanessa would sit upright in her cot like the Queen Empress lording it over her adoring subjects, talking to them in a strange weird babble. We then forbade the older children not to communicate with her in this way. Soon Vanessa was talking and acting well ahead of the norm for her age.

We really enjoyed the children. They were a delightfully happy bunch, and I think we were a wonderfully fulfilled unit.

I would have loved to have had more children but I recognised that the decision was Geraldine's to make.

Stephen Fuller with daughters (L-R) Sarah, Vanessa and Julie, 1970

CHAPTER XXIII

THE FLOOD IN SOMERSET

In 1965, we were living in Stoney Stratton, a glorious hamlet close to where I worked in the Clarks shoe factory in the small town of Shepton Mallet in the centre of Somerset. I was by now working as an Assistant Factory Manager.

We were renting a flat in the nursery wing of a 17th century Manor house. The nursery had been a small brewery in the early part of the nineteenth century before being converted into an extra wing to the main house in the latter years of Queen Victoria's reign. For our weekly rental of £7 plus my duties cutting the grass we got four bedrooms, two sitting rooms, two bathrooms, a large dining room, an enormous kitchen boasting a Rayburn solid fuel cooker and the full use of the garden.

The gardens were a joy, classic Edwardian complete with borders, croquet lawn, greenhouse, a summer house and the final glory was a red Copper Beech. However the inside of the manor house was probably very nice also but one could barely see it because of the neglected furniture and the cloak of dust.

Lady of the Manor, Mrs. Neill, had two maids and a gardener to look after the house and 2 acre garden. All of them over 70. Mrs. Neill, the gardener and the younger of the two maids looked after the garden and the older maid did both the housework and most of the cooking.

Mrs. Neill had taken a great fancy to Julie and would "borrow" her to go for long walks. In fact she looked after Julie so much that on occasion Geraldine had to ask to have her back.

When Geraldine was pregnant with Sarah we quickly realised that we would need some help. No members of our families were available to come to help out, but I needed to be out at work full time. Who was going to do the housework? Who was going to look after Julie? Who was going to do the endless washing of clothes and nappies?

I had no choice but to volunteer myself for the positions of housekeeper, maternity nurse, child minder and chief bottle washer. I then had to seek unpaid leave from my wonderful boss Roger Bostock.

Roger asked if I had any experience of the diverse skills that my proposal required. He knew what I was going to reply that I had not but I had no other option but to try. He then asked who was going to do my work overseeing the huge factory reorganisation that we were going through. He also knew my answer to that question – I did not know. Later that day he wandered up to me and suggested diffidently that:

- He would give one of the ladies in the staff canteen unofficial permission to be off ill for several weeks before the birth and some weeks after.

- The lady in question, Janet would come and help us out during her "sick leave". She would get paid by the Company and if we chose to give her a bonus, well that was up to us.

- I would take a couple of days off at the time of the birth and work short hours for the first few weeks after the birth.

It was a wonderful suggestion to which Geraldine readily agreed. She knew that Janet was a helpful and extremely competent person who had performed the same service for her own daughters and daughters-in-law. It was an easy decision to make. My known incompetence would be no match for Janet's calm and efficient skills. What could go wrong?

We found out two weeks later.

I had gone into the factory about 2 miles away to oversee some of the reorganisation and Janet had popped into the village to see one of her granddaughters knowing I would be home soon. I got a phone call from Geraldine to tell me to come home straight away because it was raining so hard that the courtyard outside the French window was starting to flood. It was only then that I noticed the sound of the rain on the factory roof. 10 minutes later when I pulled up to the house the water had risen so that it was about six inches up the glass of the French door.

By the time we got everybody and the essential baby items upstairs, the water had risen another six inches and had seeped onto the kitchen floor. The water was causing the French door to bulge so much that I opened it to prevent the flood from smashing it down.

We were trapped upstairs. The phone lines did not work. We could not see anyone. We had no idea what to do. We made various plans all of which now seem impractical. The least crazy one that I can remember was that we would use the body of the pram as a little life boat for the girls whilst Geraldine and I would swim alongside – one pushing and one pulling.

After about an hour we noticed that the water had stopped rising. I still have a vivid picture of walking in the kitchen with the water level at mid chest height and seeing some wooden ornamental clogs floating past.

Then the waters seem to subside almost as quickly as they rose. Other villagers and police appeared. Within another hour the water level in the kitchen was down to six inches and falling rapidly. Although weird things still happened. As I was walking up the tarmac drive, it appeared to sink beneath my weight. It took me a minute or two to work out what was happening – the water had got under the tarmac and was pushing it up and my boots were puncturing the tarmac and so causing it to go back down to ground level.

With very little fuss things went back to normal. The police disappeared once they had established that things were OK and that their presence was not required. No press, no TV and no dramatic pictures in the news media. We were after all in a remote part of a remote county. I believe that there was a one sentence comment in the TV Regional programme to say that the flash flood near Evercreech Junction had subsided without any serious damage.

It may not have been serious to them but it was very serious to those few of us who had experienced it. Imagine what it was like walking in four feet of water in your kitchen with your wife and two small children upstairs, not knowing what was causing it and with not another person in sight. Weird. Surreal. In retrospect, frightening.

CHAPTER XXIV

DEATH OF MY FATHER

Father invited some friends to go fishing on a Sunday afternoon in July 1973. However the friends phoned on the Saturday to say that they could not go and the boatman, having only reluctantly agreed in the first place, said that he would prefer not to go either.

Father decided he would go anyway. The boat was a wonderful 24 foot wooden yawl with an inboard diesel engine. Fully equipped with lifebelts and, in case of engine failure, wooden oars. The exterior of the boat was painted white, the interior yellow and the underneath of the boat red. Father had chosen the colours because he said that if anything ever went wrong these were the colours that could be best seen from a distance.

At about 10pm another boat hailed him. They talked about how good the fishing and weather were. Flat, calm. Not a puff of wind. Father appeared in very good form and said that he had already caught two boxes of fish. At that time of year the fish were most likely to be mackerel. Two boxes of mackerel in the fish market were considered to be 224 fish.

The other boat returned to harbour. Neither Father nor his boat ever returned to the harbour.

The fishing fleet in Union Hall and all along the coast for many miles stopped fishing and searched for him for three days. The RNLI lifeboats all along the coast did the same. Coastal Command based in Cornwall flew their long range Search and Rescue aircraft in the search. Details of the search were broadcast in the National News and in the newspapers, we had underwater searches conducted by the local diving clubs. I personally walked the cliffs for many miles East and West of the harbour. Everything that could be done was done.

Nothing was ever found.

Not a part of the wooden boat. Not a lifebelt. Not a wooden oar. Nothing.

How could this happen? I know the coast has many inlets. There are many caves and several islands but to find nothing! Father knew the area really well. He had been fishing it every year for 50 years. It seems impossible, but it happened.

It is true that he was 69 and a little overweight. If he had caught that many fish, he would have been tired. He knew almost nothing about things mechanical and certainly knew nothing about boat engines. If the engine had broken down he would not have been able to fix it. He certainly would not have been able to row such a heavy boat of that length. If by chance a fishing line had got tangled around the propeller shaft, he might have toppled over into the sea whilst trying to reach it. Although he was a good swimmer, he would not have been in any fit state to swim ashore. This is only speculation. Even that guessing does not explain why no trace of the boat was ever found.

The weather was good. Such a distinctive coloured boat would be seen for miles. Even if by some mischance the hull had been pierced, the wooden boat would have floated and must have been seen in such a detailed and diligent search.

About ten months later, the lower half of a body was found in the ocean many miles away. Mother identified it as Father because she said she recognised the underpants which had been darned in a way she darned. We buried the remains, with due ceremony in the family vault in Myross Churchyard in Union Hall. Apart from my Mother none of the family believed it was really my Father. I think perhaps Mother believed it was because she needed closure.

I remain flabbergasted and very sad. Also hugely regretful. This was a man who had so much to tell me. Many of these stories here are his.

After I left home we still saw each other every year. Geraldine, the children and I spent many of our holidays in the family home in Union Hall. Often we were there for the Summer and Christmas holidays. He and Mother visited us many times, particularly when we were living in Ireland. During my time at Trinity he would stay with me when he attended the General Synod of the Church of Ireland. We discussed things of immediate concern but we did not *really* talk, and this is what I regret.

There was a mutual understanding – when we had the time we would talk. *Really* talk. Talk not the small chat, family matters, holiday timetables and so on. We were going to have proper discussions. What do you think about serious issues? What really matters to you? What should we do together long term? Many people never have these discussions. We were going to when we had time. We never did have that time.

Many of my values come from him; from him and from my Mother. They were absorbed in things he said in passing or what he did. Many of these little stories are based on things he told almost as asides. I worked in the shop as a child and as a young man on vacation from my education. I observed him, heard what he said and heard what people said about him. I listened at the lunch table when he and Mother discussed the business and the happenings of the neighbourhood.

I regret so much that events prevented us from those having those so worthwhile experiences. Not only have I lost out but my descendants have lost out because there is so much more that I could have passed on to them.

The lesson for me is talk to those you really want to talk to. You never know when you will not be able to.

CHAPTER XXV

GERALDINE

I moved to Boylan in 1971 but we could not find a suitable house. So we decided to build one. Actually it was a bungalow.

The Church of Ireland sold us a 2.5 acre site next to the Rectory. It had been the field in which the Rectors kept their horses in days of yore. Geraldine and I with the help of the architect designed the building. I project managed and purchased all the required materials. I had a very able builder provide the direct labour. In this way we had the house we wanted built to good quality standards and at a reasonable price.

Being deep in rural Ireland Geraldine could get very capable help in the house and I could get willing help in the garden. The nearby small village of Glaslough won prizes many times in various competitions including the Tidy Towns accolade as the most beautiful well-kept small village in Ireland. I liked it even more when we added a village hall with tennis courts attached.

The girls attended the local Church of Ireland primary school in nearby Monaghan. A very good if basic education was supplied by teachers whom they and we liked.

At this time schooling in the Republic was dominated by very strict discipline and learning by rote. Pupils had to learn reams of stuff by heart. Not just poetry but essays and critiques. Getting pupils to think for themselves was rarely encouraged. Sport for girls was not considered of significant importance. Geraldine and I thought that learning by rote could be beneficial in certain circumstances but certainly not to the exclusion of thinking for oneself. Accordingly we chose boarding at the Quaker influenced Drogheda Grammar School. It was difficult for us to accept this part-time separation but we did so in the belief that we were doing the best for our children. Expensive, yes, but we believed we were doing the right thing. We missed the children hugely but we did get to see them most weekends. Also, I became a member of the Quaker Committee which ran the school, so we probably knew more than most parents about the life led by the children in a boarding school.

Another benefit for me was working closely with Quakers. I had been exposed to much of the Quaker ethos at Clarks who were a firm owned and run by Quakers – although that ethos was dwindling as time went by. Working closely with this kindly bunch of people was a pleasure. It was also a learning curve of some magnitude. Before a committee meeting we had tea and cakes, which was all gentle good humour and kindly chat. The meetings began with a minute's silence. The meeting then began and the tone changed dramatically. Still quiet gentle voices, but they stuck doggedly to their individual views until they could be persuaded otherwise. We never took a vote so there were no majority decisions. There were no minorities feeling they had been outgunned. The Chairman expressed "a feeling of the meeting" and unless this was accepted unanimously we discussed the topic again and again and – if necessary – again, until we could have a unanimous "feeling of the meeting". If we could not have unanimity we postponed the item to the next meeting. The next meeting in some mysterious way usually resolved the issue.

I learnt so much from dealing with these pleasant people. In later years, I often wished I was dealing with such people again. I was able to have the opening minute of silence in a few cases but none where "feeling of the meeting" prevailed. Pity.

The School Committee soon made me chairman of the Finance sub-committee. The school had been in a bad way financially and now we made a number of changes to cure the problem. One of the ways was regularly increasing the fees. I must have been the only person who kept on increasing the fees he had to pay.

In the autumn of 1983, all was going well. Julie had graduated from the University of Dublin. Sarah had qualified as a Chef and was working in Dingle. Nessa was approaching the end of her secondary school tenure at Drogheda Grammar School. Geraldine was directing the local Amateur Dramatic Society in Glaslough. I was working hard at a difficult time for industry generally and for the footwear manufacturing industry in particular.

One evening Geraldine and I were due to attend the Glaslough Dramatic Society end of season party at which she was due to receive a presentation. In the afternoon she said that she had a horrid headache and did I mind if we did not go to the party. Of course I agreed and we sat quietly in the lounge watching the sun go down over the garden and the hill beyond. The headache abated overnight.

I was due to go to the North East Coast of the United States of

America for work, but suggested that I would postpone it if she thought that the massive headache of the day before presaged any serious issues. She assured me today she was feeling fine and that I really should go on the trip.

I duly went to New York and the surrounding areas, ending my trip in Boston, Massachusetts. I had never been North of Boston at that time so I decided to spend Sunday exploring the coast of Maine. An early October day on the Northern Maine coast can be very bleak. From an isolated telephone box on the coast I phoned Geraldine's sister Barbara who lived in Enniskerry near Dublin where Geraldine was staying whilst I was away. Barbara was not in but I got Karen, Barbara's eldest daughter. Over a very poor line I thought I heard Karen say that Aunty Geraldine was much better now and would be out of hospital soon.

It was only later in the day that I was able to speak with Barbara who said that Geraldine had been walking down O'Connell Street with Vanessa and just fell over. Vanessa was wonderful, kept her head and, with the help of people nearby called an ambulance who took them to St. Vincent's Hospital. The hospital could find nothing wrong but had kept her in for observation.

I rushed back to Dublin but the message was repeated. Cannot find anything wrong but we must keep her in for observation. Reassured, after a couple of days I returned home and to work.

Geraldine was due to be discharged on Wednesday 20th October, and I was to pick her up. On the morning Geraldine phoned to say that her discharged had been postponed so that she could be reviewed by a specialist team, and so I was to pick her up on Thursday instead.

Reassured that the specialists had found nothing untoward, I went to the factory on Thursday morning before I was due to collect her. There I got a phone call from her Doctor to say that I was to come to Dublin straight away because "she was seriously ill".

I knew then, absolutely knew, that she was dead. So much so that I got the driver, which John Bond rightly insisted I have, to stop on the way to the hospital in Dublin so that I could collect a dark suit, white shirt and black tie.

When I got to the hospital I was told that overnight an aneurysm had burst in her brain. Technically she was still alive but on a support machine without any hope of recovery.

It was truly awful. The girls were devastated. Vanessa, always so polite, was horrendously rude to the Nun who offered her support.

Sarah literally did not say a word for three days. I was helpless, bewildered. Everything still is a horrid cold blur. Were it not for Julie I think we could not have managed - she was like a mother to us all.

Geraldine and Stephen, holding Julie

PART FIVE

1961 - 2019

CAREER

CHAPTER XXVI

GRANDAD STEPHEN JOHN FULLER AND HIS GRANDSON STEPHEN JENNINGS FULLER

I joined C & J Clark, Shoemakers of Street, Somerset, immediately after graduation in 1961 as a Graduate Trainee. Clarks was the largest and by far the most technically advanced footwear manufacturer in the World. I joined the company because of Victor Eadie. Eadie, a Kerryman, had been a prisoner-of-war of the Japanese on the infamous Burma Railroad. When we met he was a chunky 200lbs, but when he came home after the war he weighed only 82lbs. Nevertheless he had the drive and brains to become a main Board Director at Clarks.

Eadie, interviewing me in the Imperial Hotel in Cork asked what I would like to drink. When I ordered a half of Guinness he said: "I don't do halves." Several pints later I had agreed to join Clarks where he and I would drive the business forward.

Clarks, a Quaker owned and led company spent a lot of time and money training its staff at all levels. I enjoyed very much the people and the work and I learned a lot.

After 10 years I had become Factory Manager of the children's footwear division in Dundalk, Ireland. However, I realised that my wife and children were spending the money as quickly as I could earn it, and accordingly began to look for a better paid position.

In 1971 I moved to James Boylan & Son Ltd which was then a very small footwear manufacturing company. Boylan was situated in Mullan, a tiny hamlet near Emyvale in Co. Monaghan. Mullan was, in the words of the colourful founder of the company James Boylan, "the arsehole of nowhere".

Boylan, in contrast to the enormous Clarks, employed only 67 people, used out of date machinery, and in marketing terms were going nowhere. I became the Managing Director elect.

Modern agricultural machinery meant that the market for our traditional workboot was shrinking. I could see that if I added 'bells and whistles' to it could be marketed as a hiking boot.

Two years after I had joined Boylan the business was still very small. We had no additional money to be put into the company to fund marketing campaigns or hire top designers. However, we had started to grow and we had our first reasonable attempts at hiking and climbing boots.

Then we got lucky! We had enquiries from the famed Slazenger brand and indeed one of the family, Freddy Slazenger, was showing particular interest. We rushed ahead making samples which Freddy liked. He was so appreciative of our efforts and commended our approach "a brave little Irish company taking on the world." Our efforts were rewarded with what he called a *small* order of 4,000 pairs!

Small it might be to the mighty Slazenger business but to us it was huge.

Of course money was tight, however, I had the excellent training in money control from my time in Clarks and I had watched and learned from my Father. Every week I would go through the debtors with Anne Flannery, the excellent office worker and credit controller. Anne later became company secretary and managed the administration of the company very capably for many years. We noted that Slazengers had not paid for the samples. It was not a lot of money but nevertheless remember the old adage *starting as you mean to go* on I got Anne to drop a note to the Slazenger financial accounts manager.

Getting no response, I took it in my own hands to ring Freddy ever so politely and humbly. He was very decent about the whole thing, apologised for the oversight and promised to send the cheque for the samples forthwith. Regrettably the cheque never arrived and our subsequent reminders did not work either.

Then I remembered the story father had told me about his father, my grandfather Stephen John Fuller. In the early 1920s Stephen John Fuller was running the family village shops and various other little enterprises. In addition to the shops Stephen John had a small farm, was an agent selling tickets for transatlantic voyages on the Cunard line from Cobh to New York, imported coal, and had a small smokehouse for preserving fish (mostly mackerel and herring) and fishing nets using the barking process.

One day to his delight Stephen John got a letter from Albany, New York State. In this letter the writer said he had visited County Cork the month previously and had tasted some preserved fish which he was told was produced by Stephen John Fuller. Unfortunately, it was right at the end of his trip and he did not have time to visit Union Hall before his return to New York. The writer would be grateful if Stephen John Fuller would be so kind as to ship him some sample mackerel for which he enclosed $100 which he hoped would cover the shipping costs also.

A while later Stephen John was even happier to receive a letter enclosing a small order for $1000 of fish to be sent and the writer would be delighted to pay promptly when the fish arrived. So this continued with several more orders, and payment was always prompt. Stephen John was particularly pleased about the praise in the letter of the quality of his fish.

His delight was increased when he got a huge order. So huge that he had to buy in fish from others because he couldn't produce enough on his own. The colossal shipment was duly made, roughly 500 barrels of fish. His delight turned to horror and sadness when he got a cable: "Sorry to say all fish arrived rotten, please send replacements immediately."

Imagine his consternation, his businesses were at risk, he had to look up Albany on a map to see that it was upstate New York and was the capital of New York State, it was tiny compared to New York City. In 1922 there were no telephones in Union Hall (probably the nearest telephone was Cork City which was 50 miles away). He was devastated: he said later that he could not afford to replace the fish. The rest of his business was in danger. Furthermore his fish business was in jeopardy because he could not now trust his preserving process. Then he realised that there was something wrong, the process had worked for many years, and this report was out of line with what he knew to be true.

He had to find out the true story. He rode his horse to Skibbereen, took the train to Cobh and sailed to New York. Then by rail the 150 miles north to Albany.

Arriving at the address given by his customer he posed as the owner of a country grocery store and asked to see preserved fish. The salesman was delighted to show him this wonderful fish newly arrived from Ireland. You can see right there on the barrel, it was produced by S Fuller and Son Union Hall, County Cork, Ireland.

I treasure Stephen John's reply. "That is my name on the barrel. Pay me".

And so they did.

Those words from my childhood came back to me when I reviewed the invoice for a few pounds that was seriously overdue. The payment for the 4,000 pairs of boots had not been received either but that was only a few days late.

I decided not to alert Freddy Slazenger but to go to his London Office as soon as was reasonably possible. At reception I asked for Freddy giving the receptionist my card. Through the glass I could see her talking to Freddy. She came back and said that Mr Slazenger was busy, could I call later? I replied that I had plenty of time and I would wait in the café just across the street.

There I sat in the window facing their front door and for the next 3 hours. I could see Freddy if he came out of the building and I could be seen from his offices. When the three hours elapsed I returned and was shown into Freddy's office through the door on which was emblazoned in gold leaf "Frederick Slazenger, Chairman".

Freddy went straight into the attack: "Stephen, I am very hurt at your arriving unannounced like this." I said it was just a friendly call because I was in the area on other business, but as I was here, could I have payment for the samples and indeed the bulk?

Getting very agitated Freddy snarled that the quality was appalling and he was just about to send the whole lot back. I insisted that

Freddy took me to his warehouse where I could inspect the footwear, graciously offering to take the whole order back if it was faulty. Of course on reviewing the boots I could see that they were faultless. Suspicions raised, I gave instructions to the foreman to return the boots to me in Mullan forthwith.

I was very happy that within a few weeks we had sold the consignment to a Scottish customer for significantly more than we had charged Freddy.

Eight months later the sporting goods world was horrified to learn that a man posing as a member of the mighty Slazenger family had absconded, owing many suppliers large amounts of money.

CHAPTER XXVII

HERO OF THE COLD WAR

By mid 1973 the reform of Boylan was well underway. However we needed money in order to improve the business, and to get money we needed sales.

Although our new hiking boots were slowly growing in popularity, much of our income still came from the sale of our traditional farm work boots. However, we had competition. The 'Czech Boot' was a superb quality boot made in what was then called Czechoslovakia. Despite high import duty and wholesaler margins, the Czech Boot was still being sold more cheaply than our equivalent. Impossible.

The Czech Boot was clearly being dumped*, Czechoslovakia, behind the Iron Curtain**, was desperately short of Western currency and I assumed this was a way of getting it.

If we could prove that the boot was being sold for less than the cost of production or the sale price in Czechoslovakia we could stop its sale in Ireland. But how? The Irish Government had severed diplomatic relations with Czechoslovakia over a row about some Bishop, the details of which I have forgotten. The British would not help because ours was not a British company. So the answer I suggested to Jim Boylan, my Chairman, was that the next time business took me to West Germany I would go on to Czechoslovakia and buy a pair of boots. I added that I had always wanted to visit Prague, so I would take an extra few days holiday sightseeing.

I applied to the consulate in London for a visa and a few weeks

---

* Dumped meaning being sold at less than the cost of production.

** The Iron Curtain was the name for the boundary dividing Europe into two separate areas at the end of World War II in 1945 until the end of the Cold War in 1991.

later I was at Prague airport hailing a taxi. I asked the young driver to take me to the nearest department store and after considerable bureaucratic nonsense was able to buy a pair of boots similar in every detail to the boots that were hurting our business.

There was one difference, the price. In Ireland the retail price of the boot was £5, I calculated that before duty and the wholesaler's margins the retail price in Prague should be £1.82.

But it was not £1.82; it was the equivalent in Czech currency of more than £7.

It was greater than 4 times what it should have been. On this basis their price in Ireland should have been £19.23. No wonder they could afford such good materials and high labour cost. I was elated. I could now enjoy my next few days holiday knowing that I could stop these boots being dumped into our home market.

I got the taxi driver to take me to my hotel (called I think the Ambassador) in Wenceslas Square, an excellent hotel in a lovely part of a lovely city. At the end of every corridor in the bedroom area was a sort of concierge office in which sat a very alert old lady. Her job appeared to be to spy on and take detailed notes on whom the inhabitants of each room chose to have as visitors. This amused rather than concerned me.

The next day I went sightseeing and souvenir hunting. I so enjoyed the sightseeing. This was the same wonderful Prague that people are lucky enough to be able to visit today with three differences. Firstly, everything was covered in soot from the nasty smoke caused by the cheap inefficient brown coal (lignite) which seemed to be the only type of fuel available. Secondly, there was only the dimmest of public lighting and of course no neon, no advertising. Thirdly, and very noticeable, was the lack of people – no tourists, only the locals in their ill-fitting dull clothing.

The next day I resolved to be more adventurous so when it came to lunch time I sought out a back street hostelry. I sat at the bar reading up on my mornings adventures when all hell broke loose. One of the beer pumps exploded sending a flood of beer over everything. My trousers in particular. My swearing in English was picked up by my neighbour at the bar. He helped greatly by ordering towels, napkins etc. When everything calmed down I bought him a drink to thank him. We continued chatting in English and because I had bought him a drink he bought me a drink. And because he had bought me a drink I bought him a drink. And so on ad infinitum. It turned out that he was a research chemist studying amongst other things, leather, in which of course I was very interested. Much later as very good friends we swapped contact details. And so to bed.

The following evening I phoned the number given me by my newfound friend. I knew from the timbre of the voice of the man who answered that it was the same chap. However this time he had only very little English. All I could gather was that nobody of the name I gave lived at that address and that it certainly was not he. Strange.

At breakfast a fellow guest introduced himself. He told me that he was English working for Rank Xerox selling their second hand copying machines. Trudging around Eastern Europe flogging second hand copiers was not an attractive proposition for most Western salesman, though this oddball guy would have a hard time succeeding in the sales industry in the West. Luckily he seemed to thrive on the different atmosphere behind the Iron Curtain.

He took me under his wing and we had a monumental bar crawl in the bars of Prague. I went to bed a very happy if somewhat inebriated shoemaker. As I passed the crone in the concierge's office at the end of my corridor and wished her good night. I got a blank look in reply.

Strolling along the corridor towards my room I thought, '*You have done well Stephen, coming to this country behind the Iron Curtain to save the business. That phone call from this morning shows how active the Secret Police are here'.*

So musing I opened the door into my room and *BANG* - somebody fired a gun.

I came to with my head hitting something. I tried to make sense of what was happening. Somebody had taken a shot at me. There was that bang and that red flash. What was my head hitting?

But then I worked out the sequence of events, not a heroic avoidance of an assasintation attempt. The light bulb had exploded, I had jumped under the bed, and hit my head on the bedsprings!

PS Using the boots I had bought in Prague we were able eventually to get the Czechs condemned for dumping. The first case of dumping proved against the Czechoslovakian Government and the first case of dumping footwear proved anywhere in the European Union. Our work boot sales resumed and the beneficial results were shown in our accounts.

PPS My forecast that I would not be allowed back into Czechoslovakia was shown to be correct. Two years later I requested a visa for Geraldine and I to visit Czechoslovakia on holiday but was refused.

PPPS I sold for just over £4,000 some of the books (Dickens early editions in English) I had bought in Czechoslovakia for the equivalent of £4. I still have the remaining books, a 4 volume first edition "Complete works of Lord Byron" written in English, published by Baudry's European Library and printed in Paris by J.Smith, 16, Rue Montmorency, Paris. On the fly leaf it says "Including his suppressed poems"

PPPPS Years later after the fall of the Iron Wall and with a democratic government in the Czech Republic, the European Union gave me large amounts of money to help the Czech management to restructure their business so as to be competitive in the world of free trade.

Ironic; once they would not let me in and now I was getting serious money to help them.

PPPPPS Whenever I went to hail a taxi the six days I spent in Prague, the first taxi to arrive, with only one exception, was always the same driver who picked me up at the airport. Coincidence – no. A driver keen to have a Westerner who tipped reasonably by Western standards as a fare – possibly. Somebody told to keep an eye on what this strange young man was up to in Prague…?

CHAPTER XXVIII

GOING TO THE MOUNTAIN

In 1985 I was facing an emotional problem which was destroying me. I had met Anne and wanted her to marry me, but she was not prepared to come to Ireland. Although separated she was still technically married, her Father was near the end of his life, Nicholas was established in his school and Stephanie was just going starting secondary school. Anne loved her job as a General Practitioner in suburban Wilmslow and hated the possibility of being a General Practitioner in rural Ireland. There was, reasonably, no way she could or would leave England to move to Glaslough.

I was alone in a large bungalow, with a time consuming garden and a very needy (if beautiful) Irish Red Setter named Jed. I was really depressed. What had previously interested me no longer did.

The only good thing was the children. But they were almost grown: Julie 24 living in England, Sarah 22 living in the far away Southernmost tip of Ireland and Nessa 18 months into a 'six month break' to tour the world.

Then I had a brainwave. "If the mountain won't come to Mohammed, Mohammed *could* go to the mountain" Even though, at 46, I considered myself unemployable in a good job outside the footwear industry, I could sell up, get a minor job and this, with my savings would enable me to live in England again. Perhaps not in the style in which I would like but nevertheless a very good life with Anne.

Luckily for me, Anne agreed to marry me and I moved to Wilmslow in September 1985.

I quickly got a minor job which I did not enjoy at all. It was during a meeting with my pension provider that a new opportunity arose, he asked "how is this semi-retirement of yours going Stephen?" to which I replied that the marriage was great but the rest was not. He offered to introduce me to a friend who was deputy Chief Executive of Smurfit Management Consultant Services, Rex Lawrence. I really liked Rex and I loved the work.

Within a year I was Director UK and working six days a week.

Smurfit Group, the gigantic Irish company had huge paper production industries in many parts of the world plus their own Bank, Insurance Company, SMCS Management Consultancy and a variety of other subsidiaries. Most of the business of SMCS was outside the group. I found that my general management skills learned over the years plus SMCS training tutored by the wonderful Rex enabled me to succeed in this new-to-me environment. I did projects in a huge number of industries of widely varying disciplines mostly in the UK but occasionally abroad. I have enough material to write a book on the Do's And Don't's of my SMSCS consultancy activities. However that is not what Grandad's Little Stories is about. Suffice to say that I worked in over 70 companies, from hotels, car hire, building, paper, box making, tool manufacture, education, industry restructuring, cotton spinning, towel manufacture, garment production, and printing to name a few!

After working at SMCS for five years, an increasing number of clients began to say they loved my work but the fees were too expensive. Thus I decided to set up my own Management Consultancy - SJF Management Ltd. whose sole employee would be me and the Company Secretary would be Anne. I could now charge twice what SMCS paid me and charge the client only half of what SMCS charged them.

Most of my work was funded by the World Bank and the European Union. This meant projects in many countries. I would only accept assignments which allowed me to come home to Wilmslow every three weeks. Modern air travel and computer technology made this feasible. Three weeks' field work and meetings and then home to write it up. Some projects lasted a few months, Cyprus three years.

A lovely period of my life. Gone were the long days and driving determination which got Boylan to survive and then prosper. Now I could enjoy a wonderful home life, plus foreign travel and a satisfying job. Slowing down but nevertheless contributing. When my age slowed me down and foreign travel became a test rather than enjoyment, I began to work part time and only in the UK.

So retirement at 79 and the time to finish this "letter" to people of the future. I so hope that you enjoy it.

EPILOGUE

I AM HAPPY NOW II

I am happy now. I am 80 years old. I had my 80th Birthday Party a few days ago. 21st February 2019. We had a party and family sleeping overnight. Such fun. So many hugs. So many reminiscences.

Family started arriving on Thursday and stayed until Sunday.

Great food. Good wine. Real beer. Not too much alcohol but enough to loosen tongues.

Endless talk. Much laughter. Whilst the adults chatted and helped out the young played on the swings and kicked a football in the back garden. Even the weather celebrated - we had the best four days in the hottest February on record.

I received lots of lovely presents. I had asked that there be nothing expensive but people gave me some very lovely ingenious things. Interesting books (one I have nearly finished already: *Factfulness - ten reasons we're wrong about the world and why things are better than you think*) I get so bored with the media highlighting only bad news. This book gives me the facts to show that the world has improved so much during my lifetime. The truth is that whilst things can always get better, most aspects of life have improved enormously.

I invited only immediate family to celebrate with myself and Anne; my three children and seven of their children. Then Anne's two children and their two children (who call me Grandad to my great delight). Plus several spouses. 19 people in all. We did not include my brothers nor their children. Not because we did not want them but the house was full to bursting! We will have other parties; with them when we visit Union Hall in July. And with friends and neighbours in Wilmslow.

The older I get the more I enjoy people. And these truly are wonderful people.

Stephen Fuller with all of his grandchildren
Sadhbh, Tess, Alannah, Dara, Murray, Dylan, Leah, and Stephen
September 2017

APPENDICES

i   The Fullers and the Moxelys

This is a brief summary of what I know or find interesting about my antecedents. My dictionary defines antecedents as "a person's ancestors and social background". By antecedents I mean a combination of what I know and think about my ancestors that I find interesting. Strict historical data is given in the family tree in the back of this book.

FATHER

Noel Stephen Fuller was born on January 2, 1906. Hence the Noel. The Stephen was because his father was Stephen and his father's father was Stephen. Indeed Stephen is a Fuller family first name going back many many years. Usually called Noel he always liked to sign himself either NS Fuller or Noel Stephen Fuller because he wanted the continuity of the name Stephen. Father had a quiet pride in the family. I share that quiet belief in the family.

Like his brothers, Father was educated first by a home tutor and then at the Irish equivalent of a public school, Methodist College in Belfast, Methody as he always called it. However unlike his brothers, Father stayed in County Cork. Tom had gone on to being something in the Establishment in Northern Ireland and Bill to various posts in the British Establishment as either a member of the Colonial Service in Africa and the Middle East and as an executive (at one time Company Secretary) of the Anglo-Iranian Oil Company. Father thought others saw him as *just a shopkeeper in the South of Ireland.*

The above paragraph is true and it yet is not the whole truth. Bill and Tom did hold those posts but the reality was that they were middle rankers. The truth about Father is that he was highly respected in whichever circle he was, including his brothers. He was an important personage in his Union Hall centred community. His customers and suppliers looked upon him as a man of integrity. Many sought his advice on all sorts of quasi-legal matters affecting their families. On a number of occasions I heard customers address him as "Father" a term reserved for the most highly respected man in the community - the Parish Priest. In his business dealings he was regarded as a man of his word who could be trusted. For many years he was a member of the General Synod (parliament) of the Church of Ireland for the whole of Ireland, as well as being a member of the Diocesan Synod for Cork, Cloyne and Ross.

At 5 feet 8 tall Father was shorter than all his three sons; Stuart 6ft

2, me 6ft and Stanley 5ft 10ish. He was only somewhat tubby, which is extraordinary when one considers the enormous quantity of food he ate. He liked food so much that at the end of dinner he and Mother would discuss in detail the next day's dinners. When we went fishing he used to bring out the food hampers soon after we cleared the harbour. He then produced chocolate bars or biscuits to keep us going until we had our real picnic later. This almost always caused Gerry Baker, our boatman to say "Your God is your belly" which greatly amused us boys.

I know he considered that he had a hard working hard life. But pause and think. Yes, he did work long hours. The shop was open from 9 in the morning until 8 at night. However the shop was closed for lunch from 1pm-2pm every day and it was closed for Bank and many Church Holidays. He did not have to be in the shop all the time. For example he was quite often away on church business. In Summer we went fishing at least three often four afternoons a week. In the shooting seasons we were often out two or three times a week. His work, nearly always, was pleasant whether dealing with customers or suppliers. Almost never did he have the pressure or the confrontations which I have observed in business. I say almost never, it may have been never because although we were very close from when I was a child helping in the shop to when I left University I never did see confrontation or pressure in his life. His business activities were more efficient than most and he did not step outside what he knew well.

At least some of his feeling of being hard by done was because he resented being summoned back from Methody at age 17 to train to run the business, because his incredibly dictatorial Grandmother had decided that her son Stephen, Father's father, was not well enough to run the business. He never told me why but I think that it was a case of "the grass is always greener on the other side". He had not been consulted, he was just told and that is not a good way to manage people. Apart from anything else he had just been picked for the rugby First XV and all the Fullers will know how important that must have been to him.

However he did his best in the business and he had a reasonably good time as a carefree young man. Photographs show him on what looks like some good holiday cruises.

It was then that he developed his shooting and fishing hobbies. Shooting led to his losing an eye but gaining a wife, and fishing led to his death. Both of which I have described earlier in the book.

Father's way of relaxing was to play the piano. Unfortunately, because of my tone deafness, I don't know if he was any good or not; I suspect not. Also unfortunately he appeared to know only hymn tunes. So he would sing along loudly to his own piano accompaniment. I always made myself scarce during such activity.

MOTHER

Martha Jennings was born in Benduff near to Rosscarberry in 1907. I do not know the given name of her father (a farmer) but her mother was called Ann. Mother was the eldest child. Then came Eddie, Nancy (called Nance), May, Dick, Jack, Bill, Bernie and Carrie. Nine in all, Wow!

My Mother's parents lived in a lovely farmhouse in Skeafe near Bandon. It had a really big well-built set of farm buildings around a large farm square yard and about 170 acres of excellent Bandon valley fertile soil. The story goes that when Eddie the oldest son was getting married, his father decided to buy him a farm. In those days of the dreadful Depression in the mid-1930s farmland prices had dropped by an amazing amount. So they were able to buy a much bigger and more productive farm with the amount of money that they were intending to spend. When Grandpa Jennings realised that the new farm was better than the existing farm he had, he decided to give the existing farm at Benduff to Eddie and he kept the big farm for himself. I have no knowledge of what Eddie thought of this but I never remember seeing him at Skeafe and we did visit a lot. I am delighted to say, however, that Eddie did visit us in Union Hall and was a good customer as well as a good friend to my parents.

I know nothing of Mother's education and I do not know why not. However she became a nurse in the Victoria Hospital in Cork. I think she was a Sister there when Father arrived having lost one eye. Romance followed, then marriage, then me. I can add very little to what I have said elsewhere. However I can only say that she was a wonderful Mum. Brooked no nonsense but helpful, kind, efficient, and very skilled in all things to do with homebuilding. Plus she was a very good partner to my father in the business.

GRANDFATHER JENNINGS

I know almost nothing about Mother's father. When I was about four I remember him as being a little old man dressed in dark clothes, sitting in the corner of the big kitchen in Skeafe near Bandon. It appeared to me that "he was waiting to die". This he did shortly after.

One thing about Grandpa Jennings was that he had a fine head of hair. This meant that my brothers and I have not gone bald, because it is from one's mother that a man inherits the tendency to baldness. The mother inherits that baldness gene from her father. Thank you, Grandpa Jennings.

GRANDMOTHER JENNINGS

Mother's mother Ann nee Kingston was a short plump lady with the same coloured auburn hair which I had as a youngster. She bustled about. Always doing things. Surrounded by her three daughters Mother and May and Carrie both then unmarried, I could see that she clearly loved and was loved by them. The purpose of much of the bustling was the feeding and generally looking after of the men-folk of the house, her husband and sons Dick, Jack and Bernie, when I was little. Always happy she was forever hugging and generally spoiling me, her eldest grandson. Thinking about her brings to my mind a picture of a robin hopping from place to place always with a purpose and a kindly eye.

I am not certain but I believe she came from a family who lived on Sherkin Island, but brother Stuart thinks it was "somewhere beyond Drimoleague".

GRANDMOTHER FULLER

Father's mother was born Anne Elizabeth Vickery in 1873 in New Mill, Rosscarbery. I have talked about elsewhere in the book but I would like to describe her here also. Although I do not remember her ever smiling she was kind and attentive to me in the way I imagine a nanny to an upper class family in the old days might behave towards her charges. She corrected my pronunciation when I read to her. I read at first from my children's books and comics and then as I got older from the Bible and the religious magazines she had delivered. In her presence, I had to sit, walk and talk properly.

Considered by many to be a very good looking lady, she dressed always in black in predominantly silk. Long skirt, long sleeves, blouse buttoned to the neck, hair in a bun, she walked and sat in a very upright manner. She was a strong Methodist of the sombre kind. Looking back, I think that she disapproved of the non-Methodist women Uncles Tom and Bill and Father married: all of whom, goodness knows, were very upright, responsible citizens. I cannot think that anyone would have disapproved of my mother but I think that grandmother gave the impression that she did.

My grandmother Fuller must have been heavily burdened by having to look after her youngest child, Doris. Doris, not nearly as intelligent as her siblings, suffered from epilepsy and was quite child-like. Doris died at age 32 leaving grandmother even more retiring and unsmiling.

GRANDFATHER FULLER

I do not remember my grandfather, Stephen John Fuller, born in 1868, the second son. He died in December 1940 when I was not yet two years old. I cannot say why but I have always felt a great affinity for him. Perhaps it is the sharing of initials, SJF. He did leave me one of the only two bequests I have ever had, £100 in War Bonds which, when I cashed them in 1965, yielded me £28 after expenses.

Grandfather's elder brother Tom was supposed to take over the business when their incredibly strong willed mother Anne died. However Tom was also very strong willed which meant that when he clashed with his mother "sparks flew".

A good looking man, Tom was reputed to be quite a man for the ladies. When his mother discovered that he had been somewhat over friendly with one of the local girls, the sparks really flew and he had to flee to America. After some time, peace was restored and Tom came back from America to Union Hall. It was then that he had the imposing 4 story store across the way from the shop built.

However the peace did not last and he moved away from his mother and Union Hall again. This time he moved only 6 miles to Skibbereen. There he founded the very successful hardware store and builders suppliers which later on passed to his son Tom. This Tom Fuller we boys called Uncle Tom Skibbereen (to distinguish him from Father's oldest brother whom we called Uncle Tom Belfast because, not surprisingly, he lived in Belfast).

Stephen John Fuller had grown up thinking that his older brother Tom would take over the family business, which suited him very well because he really wanted to be an architect of some sort. He chose Naval Architecture and attended the relevant college in Queenstown (now Cobh). After his brother Tom had walked out of the Union Hall business for a second time, their mother summoned Stephen back from Queenstown to run the business. He protested but it was useless. One did not oppose his mother, the redoubtable

Anne.

Indeed when he was in his sixties, his bedroom was beside that of his mother. He liked to sleep in, but when he eventually got up and walked past his mother's door she would hear him. She always called out "Stephen, is that you? You should have been up long ago attending to the business". Eventually he hit on a solution. Every weekday morning he had one of the workmen put a ladder up to his bedroom window and he climbed down in peace. As a boy I placed a ladder against the window sill and climbed down just to prove it could be done.

My father had been brought home from Methody in 1924 when he was 17 years old. At that time the family did not have a motor car. Indeed most families did not. When eventually his father Stephen John was persuaded to buy a car, he asked "What is the best car available?" he was told Armstrong-Siddeley. "Right" he said "we'll have one of those". Father was delighted.

GREAT-GRANDFATHER FULLER

Thomas Stephen Fuller was born in Brinny near Bandon in 1823 to a farming family. I have no hearsay knowledge of the family and have done no worthwhile research on the family. These writings are about anecdotes and things and things that I find interesting and/or amusing. They are not about history. However I would like to know more about his parents and I hope to learn more about them.

Tom Fuller was a private tutor in Castletownshend about 3 miles from Union Hall when he met and married Anne Moxley of Union Hall. They had four children: Thomas, Elizabeth (who died in infancy), Annie and Stephen John.

GREAT-GRANDMOTHER FULLER

My great-grandmother Anne Moxley was born in Union Hall in 1828. I know little of her parents other than that her father was a shoemaker. I think she did not have any siblings.

 Her father had two brothers, both of whom died childless. At the time of her marriage, Anne worked in her uncle's small grocery shop. When her uncle died Anne inherited his business. I presume that she also inherited the worldly goods not only of her father but also those of her Moxley uncles. By the time her husband Tom died in 1869 aged 46 she had built up the business considerably.

The little grocery shop was now a bigger well stocked enterprise

The arrangements for her husband's funeral were a cause of some disagreements between his wife Anne and his parents (whom Anne called the Brinny Fullers). Anne wished him to be buried in the churchyard of the Union Hall where they worshipped. The Brinny Fullers wanted him to be buried in their family churchyard, some 30 miles away, in Ballymoney near Bandon. Apparently there were some other disagreements which ended with them barely speaking to one another.

On the day of the funeral the procession proceeded slowly towards the church yard of the Union Hall Church of Ireland where a grave had been prepared. However when it was supposed to turn left to go to the Union Hall churchyard, the hearse and the carriages containing the Brinny Fuller mourners – which were leading the procession – turned right, increased speed and kept going until they reached the Ballymoney churchyard near the Fuller family farm There he was buried with due ceremony. The Moxley mourners and, especially, Great-Grandmother were completely baffled and bewildered and chaos ensued. I believe they went to the prepared graveside where they held an impromptu service.

Bewilderment turned to rage when they returned to the house

behind the shop to discover that the Brinny Fullers had stripped the shop of the most valuable goods, including the hams that were hung on great big hooks in the ceiling to mature as was the custom in those days. The goods had been taken away to the Brinny Fullers' farm.

When Father told me this tale he cautioned me to consider the story with great care. For instance, he said that in those days a woman's belongings became the property of her husband when they married. He reminded me that *history is written by the survivors* and added that he had first heard the story about 1918, nearly 50 years after the event, when he was 12. However it is definitely true that Thomas Stephen Fuller is buried in the Old Ballymoney graveyard. My cousin Binnie Atkins and I visited there in 2012 and took photographs of the headstone.

In 1869 Anne was a widow aged 41 with three children aged 11, 3 and 1. Her shop had been deprived of its most valuable stock. We do not know for certain how much cash she had but Father thought that she did not have much. Helped by her son Tom when he grew older, she worked very hard and intelligently to build the business.

Apparently she was a woman of clear insight and great determination. She was so determined in fact that she would not tolerate second best from herself or anyone else. According to Father she was respected by many but loved by few. So determined to succeed that when son Tom left home after another row with his Mother she overruled Stephen John's desire to be a naval architect and made him come home to help her run the business. She was also so desirous of having her own way that she did not even consult her grandson, my father when she needed him to leave school at age 17 to help her run the business. Father was given no option. Against his will, he started working in the business in 1924.

We do not know in detail how she ran business but we do know that the business was sufficiently profitable that she was able to give considerable amounts of money to her daughter Annie (Eliza) on her first marriage to John Deane and later to their daughter Annie (Winnie). She gave even more money to Eliza on Eliza's marriage to Thomas John (Lord Tom) Kingston.

As a small boy I thought I had a relative in the aristocracy because everybody referred to Tom Kingston as Lord Tom on account of his "airs and graces". I thought he really was a Lord. In my innocence, when I first went away to school, I told some other boys that I had a relative who was a British Lord. Their awe soon turned to jeering and I had to ask Father what the real situation was.

The business grew to the extent that they were chartering coasters to import coal and slate from Wales. This was unloaded at Kilbeg less than a mile from Union Hall. They built a large store and a jetty at the island in Leap where niece Jean now has her lovely house. The smaller coasters would discharge part of its load in Kilbeg and take the rest to Leap, 2 miles away via the opening bridge. The larger ships would discharge all at Union Hall and part of the cargo would be transhipped to Leap using smaller vessels. This importation was still going on in the 1950s. I remember well getting incredibly covered in coal dust when playing near the unloading of the coal boats in Kilbeg.

The business was prospering to the extent that all of Stephen John's children had private tutoring until they went away to the Irish equivalent of minor public schools. The three sons Father, Tom and Bill to Methodist College, Belfast and Nancy and Mabel went to Wesley College, Dublin. Doris was considered to be incapable of withstanding the rigours of boarding school.

Anne was thriving well into her 90s. On one occasion a customer asked her son Stephen John how his mother was. He replied well. According to Stephen John the customer said "I expect the good

God isn't ready for her yet". He then had a vision of God up in Heaven cowering at the thought of the bossy Anne Fuller telling him what to do.

Stephen Fuller and Annie (nee Vickery), my paternal Grandparents

ii The Fuller Shop through the ages

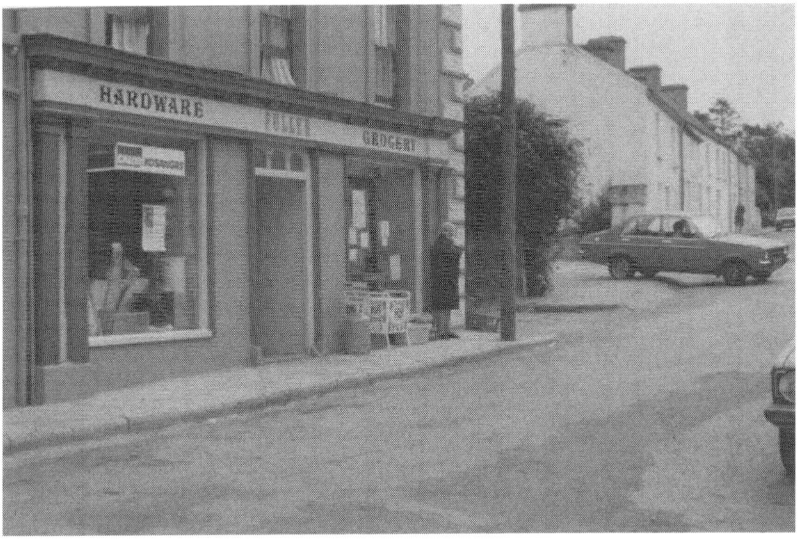
HARDWARE
GROCERY

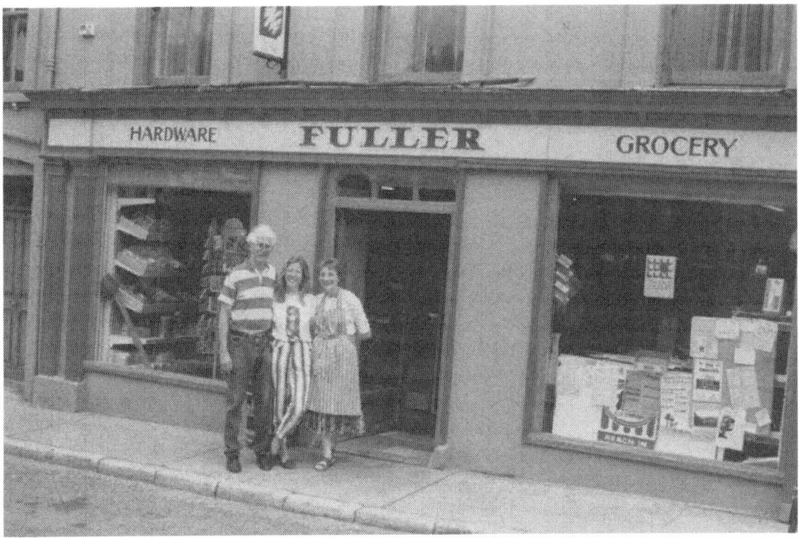
HARDWARE
FULLER
GROCERY

iii   Timeline of Stephen Fuller's life

21st February 1939	Stephen Jennings Fuller born
1941	Stuart Fuller born
1942	Stanley Fuller born
1945	Stephen begins primary school
1947	Stephen begins Bandon Grammar school
1956	Stephen begins Mountjoy school
1957	Stephen begins Trinity College Dublin
1961-1971	Stephen works at Clarks
1961	Moves to Glastonbury, England
1962	Stephen and Geraldine marry
1963	Julie born to Stephen and Geraldine
1965	Sarah born to Stephen and Geraldine
1966	Moves to Dundalk, Ireland
1967	Vanessa born to Stephen and Geraldine
1971-1985	Stephen works at James Boylan & Sons ltd
1975	Stephen's father dies - disappeared at sea
1983	Geraldine dies
1985	Stephen and Anne marry
1985	Moves to Wilmslow, England
1985-2018	Works at Smurfit Consultancy
1988	Stephen's mother dies
1989	Tess born to Sarah and Tommy
1990	Dara born to Julie and Alan
1994	Stephen Ray born to Julie and Alan
1994	Sadhbh born to Sarah and Tommy
1996-2014	Sets up and runs SJF Management
1997	Leah born to Julie and Alan
2001-2019	Works as Chairman of IBT Group
2003	Dylan born to Vanessa and Niall
2008	Murray and Alannah born to Vanessa and Niall
2009	Meghan born to Stephanie and Hugh
2011	Harry born to Stephanie and Hugh
2019	Stephen retires
2019	Celebrates 80th birthday with family

Acknowledgements

Writing this book has been a joyful experience, full of such happy memories that came flooding back. Memories of people and places full of wit and beauty.

My thanks are due to my wonderful family and the people in the community with whom I grew up. I so enjoyed it. Thank you.

I had help and expertise from many people along the way, my friends and colleagues at the writers club, in particular Robert Bisset. My grandson Stephen Ray who enhanced and colourised many of my photographs of people and places. And my talented granddaughter Leah Jane who drew the front cover design as my 80th birthday present.

However it would not have been published without the help and determination of my wonderful granddaughter Dara Geraldine and her husband Jamie, who provided the endless hours of work that was required to put the book into print. Thank you both.

Printed in Great Britain
by Amazon